Mamaindé Stress
The Need for Strata

Summer Institute of Linguistics and
The University of Texas at Arlington
Publications in Linguistics

Publication 122

Editor

Donald A. Burquest
University of Texas
at Arlington

Consulting Editors

Doris A. Bartholomew
Pamela M. Bendor-Samuel
Desmond C. Derbyshire
Robert A. Dooley
Jerold A. Edmondson

Austin Hale
Robert E. Longacre
Eugene E. Loos
Kenneth L. Pike
Viola G. Waterhouse

Mamaindé Stress
The Need for Strata

David Eberhard

A Publication of
The Summer Institute of Linguistics
and
The University of Texas at Arlington
1995

©1995 by the Summer Institute of Linguistics, Inc.
Library of Congress Catalog No: 95–67930
ISBN: 1–55671–003–8
ISSN: 1040–0850

Printed in the United States of America
All Rights Reserved

No part of this publication may be reproduced, stored in a retrieval system, or transmitted in any form or by any means—electronic, mechanical, photocopy, recording, or otherwise—without the express permission of the Summer Institute of Linguistics, with the exception of brief excerpts in journal articles or reviews.

Cover design by Hazel Shorey

Copies of this and other publications of the Summer Institute of Linguistics may be obtained from
International Academic Bookstore
7500 W. Camp Wisdom Road
Dallas, TX 75236

I dedicate this initial attempt of mine at understanding the Mamaindé language to those who understand it best: the Mamaindé people themselves.

I also wish to pay tribute to their leader, Capitão Pedro, who died from a gunshot wound on August 13, 1993, while this monograph was still being written. Up until the time of his death, he was a major force in the protection of Mamaindé land from the constant onslaught of invading lumbermen. Now that he is gone, my prayer is that somehow God would spare this language, this culture, and above all, this people from any further tragedy and needless destruction.

Contents

Acknowledgements ix

Map x

1. Introduction 1
   1.1 Setting 1
   1.2 Linguistic classification 1
   1.3 Purpose 2
   1.4 Source of data 2
   1.5 Limitations 3
   1.6 Overview 3

2. The Mamaindé Syllable 5
   2.1 Syllable structure 5
   2.2 Syllable weight 9
   2.3 Licensing theory 12
      2.4–2.6 Licensing in Mamaindé
   2.4 The primary licenser 14
   2.5 The secondary licenser—coda 15
   2.6 The secondary licenser—appendix 19
   2.7 The completed Mamaindé syllable 21
   2.8 Syllabification 22

3. The Data and the Problem 27
   3.1 The phonetics of Mamaindé stress 27
   3.2 Basis of stress 28

3.3 The data 29
3.4–3.7 The Problem
3.4 Problem 1. Unpredictable word level stress 30
3.5 Problem 2. Unstressed heavy syllables 32
3.6 Problem 3. Light syllables which receive stress 32
3.7 Problem 4. Lengthened vowels in underlying forms 32
3.8 Methodology 33
3.9 Theory power 33

4. A Previous Solution 35
   4.1 Levels of stress 35
   4.2 Application of Kingston's stress rules 37
   4.3 Problems with the morphological stress rules 38
   4.4 Quantity sensitivity 40
   4.5 Syllable position 41

5. An Overview of Metrical Phonology 45
   5.1 Arboreal theory 45
   5.2 Grid theory 49

6. A Metrical Analysis of Mamaindé Stress 53

7. An Overview of Lexical Phonology 57

8. A Lexical Analysis of Mamaindé Stress 63
   8.1 The lexical strata 63
   8.2–8.3 The Lexical Rules
   8.2 Rules of the lexical component 69
   8.3 Rules of the postlexical component 73

9. Derivations 93

10. Metrical Trees versus Metrical Grids 123
    10.1 Practical considerations 123
    10.2 Theoretical implications 132

11. Well-Formedness Statements 135

Appendix: A Comparative Study of Indigenous Brazilian
   Stress Systems 143

References 155

Acknowledgements

I would like to express my appreciation to those who have made possible this volume which is the outcome of my graduate studies for a master's degree. First of all, I am grateful to the members of my graduate committee who made numerous suggestions and gave helpful advice throughout the writing process. I am particularly indebted to Dr. Donald Burquest, for introducing to me in the classroom the theories presented here, pointing my writing in the right direction, and challenging me to constantly improve it through his keen observations, patient editing, and timely encouragement.

A word of special thanks also to Peter Kingston who first introduced me to the Mamaindé language and people. Without the considerable amount of previous work done by Kingston on this language, this book could never have been written. In particular, his *Pedagogical Grammar of Mamaindé,* his *Mamaindé-Portuguese Dictionary,* and his help in glossing texts have been invaluable to me.

I am also indebted to my wife, Julie, who gave me the time to be able to complete this paper. She has willingly filled in for me at home, putting up with my many long days and late nights of time away from the family. She has also been a tremendous help in pointing out errors and discrepancies that needed to be corrected in the manuscript. She has my total admiration.

Lastly, I thank the Mamaindé people themselves, who have been very willing and gracious teachers of their language.

1
Introduction

1.1. Setting. Mamaindé is the language spoken by a group of approximately 120 Mamaindé Indians in west-central Brazil. This group is located on the Guapore Valley Reserve, in the state of Mato Grosso, just south of the town of Vilhena, and between the confluences of the Cabixi and Pardo rivers. The Mamaindé language community lives for the most part in one single village which goes by the name of Capitão Pedro. A related lect, known as Negaroté, is spoken in a neighboring village by some forty to fifty individuals. This study, however, focuses exclusively on the Mamaindé spoken in the village of Capitão Pedro.

1.2. Linguistic classification. The Mamaindé language is referred to by most scholars as Northern Nambiquára, and has been classified as a member of the Nambiquára linguistic family (McQuown and Greenberg 1960; Rodrigues 1986). It is one of the smaller language families in Brazil, with only two other members: Southern Nambiquára and Sabané. Affiliation of this family itself to a phylum seems very tentative at this point, as opinions vary considerably. McQuown and Greenberg (1960) and Voegelin and Voegelin (1977) place the Nambiquára languages in the Je-Pano-Carib phylum, whereas Kaufman (1990) considers them to be of Macro-Tucanoan stock. Aryon Rodrigues (1986), on the other hand, considered by many to be the leading authority on Brazil's native languages, makes no attempt to classify Nambiquára any further, characterizing it as an isolated language family. This opinion is also shared by Ribeiro (1957).

1.3. Purpose. In the Mamaindé language, the stress system is the basis upon which much of the phonology and morphology rests.[1] Many of the phonological rules apply only in stressed environments. Other prosodic features of Mamaindé, such as nasalization, laryngealization, tone,[2] reduplication, and intonation must also appeal to the presence of the stressed element. Even in such simple morphological matters as the affixation of person markers, reference to stress is necessary in order to choose the correct morpheme.[3] It becomes quickly apparent that a detailed study of stress is crucial for a better understanding of this language.

The purpose of this volume is twofold. On the practical level, it is to make a tentative statement which can predict the placement of Mamaindé stress by using the tools available within current metrical theory.

Secondly, I also attempt to accomplish a more theoretical purpose in this study which is to give support to the theory of lexical phonology, using Mamaindé as an example of a language which must use several strata within the phonology in order to account for stress.

Some corollary points are also made which I feel merit attention at the outset: (1) The Mamaindé data gives us evidence from a specific language that supports the grid theory over the arboreal theory within the framework of metrical phonology, and (2) Well-formedness statements are shown to provide a useful means by which an intricate stress system like Mamaindé can be understood in the light of universal phonological processes.

1.4. Source of data. I gathered the data for this volume from Mamaindé speakers in the village of Capitão Pedro while on numerous visits to the reserve during the years 1990 through 1992 under the auspices of the Summer Institute of Linguistics. Text material, one long text and one short text, was recorded on tape and then transcribed both

---

[1] This also appears to be the case in Southern Nambiquára, where the stress rule is considered to precede all other rules (Kroeker 1972).

[2] Mamaindé is a tonal language with two register tones and two contour tones. Much valuable work by Kingston has been done in this area ("Tonal Curves and Perturbation in Mamaindé," "Tonal Configuration and Perturbation in Mamaindé"). Although some connections have been found between the tonal system and the stress system, they have been minor. However, it is possible that by viewing tone as an autosegment, there may be a greater link established between the placement of stress and tone sandhi. This topic needs further study.

[3] For example, the first person subject marker is -*ax* after a stressed syllable, and -*nax* after an unstressed syllable.

Introduction

phonetically and in the Mamaindé orthography developed by Peter Kingston. The language consultant for the longer text was Donaldo Mamaindé, while the shorter text was from Luiz Cabeção Mamaindé. Some stress patterns were analyzed with the help of CECIL software (Computer Extracted Components of Intonation in Language). Kingston's help was invaluable in the orthographic transcription of these texts. Also used as a data reference was the Mamaindé-Portuguese dictionary (Kingston 1991a).

1.5. Limitations. The actual time I spent in the language community was very restricted due to factors beyond my control. Each visit to the Mamaindé village was limited to no more than two or three days. Because of this, my lack of expertise in the language must be taken into account when considering the analysis here. Therefore, this is in no way intended to be a definitive statement regarding the rules determining the placement of stress in Mamaindé.

Time did not permit an exhaustive instrumental analysis of every word in the database, so the actual placement of stress on the majority of the data is based on my own judgment and auditory impression.

1.6. Overview. I first describe the Mamaindé syllable since stress is directly related to syllable structure and weight. This is done using a three-dimensional model of syllable structure.

Second, I briefly describe the phonetic reality of Mamaindé stress.

In the third chapter the crucial data is presented, and the problem of characterizing stress in this language is detailed.

I then consider three attempts to describe the Mamaindé stress system, beginning with Kingston's analysis in chapter 4, moving on to metrical theory in chapters 5 and 6, and finally combining a metrical analysis with lexical phonology in chapters 7 and 8. This last analysis is the one I propose as the most adequate so far. Brief chapters on both metrical and lexical theory precede each analysis in order to clarify terms and theoretical differences.

Chapter 9 demonstrates the usefulness of the analysis developed in the previous chapter by showing detailed derivations of almost every type of word found in the language.

Alternative metrical formalisms are considered in chapter 10; I argue that an approach using metrical grids is more adequate in characterizing Mamaindé stress than that using metrical trees.

Finally, in chapter 11, I propose a series of well-formedness conditions as an attempt to explain the universal motivations behind the language-specific stress rules found in Mamaindé.

The appendix provides a quick comparative look at other stress systems found within Brazil, particularly those among the Amazonian languages, to investigate precisely where Mamaindé fits in. As far as I know, this is the first such comparative listing of the stress systems and stress rules found in the different language families of Brazil.

2
The Mamaindé Syllable

Any adequate description of Mamaindé stress must first include a description of the structure of the syllable, which in Mamaindé is the domain of stress placement. I do not, however, attempt to describe every detail of the Mamaindé syllable. Instead, I look only at those topics which are most pertinent to the discussion of stress, namely, syllable structure, syllable weight, licensing, and syllabification.

2.1. Syllable structure. The Mamaindé syllable can be characterized by the following syllable structure diagram:

(1) Mamaindé syllable structure

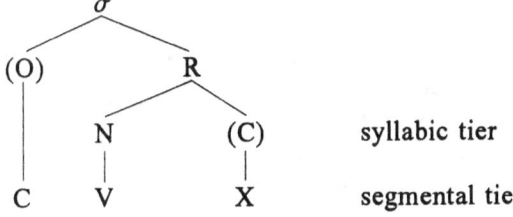

Here σ represents the SYLLABLE NODE, O the ONSET, R the RHYME, N the NUCLEUS, and C the CODA position (which is a different type of symbol from the C of the segmental tier, which represents any consonant). Also on the segmental tier, the specification X represents any single segment at all, whether a vowel or a consonant. Parentheses show that both the onset and the coda positions are optional. This syllable tree, then, permits only the syllable types shown in (2) and (3).[4]

(2) Light syllables (those without codas)

V	-a	(article)
	i-	(causative)
CV	-ta	'to me'
	-xna	(stative)
	yai-	reduplicated prefix of the root yaiyaik 'type of nut'

(3) Heavy syllables (those with codas)[5]

VX	ãn-	'to kill'
	aut-	'different'
CVX	set-	'to speak'
	hain-	'to sing'
	hainx-	'crown'
	xsin-	'to shoot at'
	wa:-	'to come'
	xai:-	'to go'

Notice that both pre- and postglottalized consonants (those preceded or followed by an *x*) are considered to be only one segment in length, not two. Taking this approach greatly simplifies the phonology in many ways, allowing broader generalizations to be made in the rules. For example, the reduplicating rule in Mamaindé, using the autosegmental template proposed by Marantz (1982), would have to construct two templates, CCVX and CVX, to account for the possibility of two positions in the onset. On the other hand, by considering the glottalized consonants to be a single segment, we can capture the reduplicating process of Mamaindé with one single template, CVX. (The X segment is

---

[4]All the examples here are single morphemes. This is a bit artificial since Mamaindé is extremely polysynthetic and allows very few unbound morphemes. For the present, however, single morphemes are used to show syllable types more clearly.

[5]A colon represents a lengthened vowel and a period a syllable boundary; nasalization is shown by a tilde over the vowel and laryngealization by underlining the vowel; *x* is the orthographic symbol used for the glottal stop in Mamaindé. For a full listing of Mamaindé phonemes, see (11) in §2.4.

The Mamaindé Syllable 7

pre-associated to the feature [−cons].) The following exemplify this reduplication pattern:

(4) yaya 'to be dead'
  kakãn 'to be gummy'
  walalãn 'to be light-weight'
  xsixsin 'to drag (pl.)'

(See Eberhard 1992, for further details.)

There are other syllables in the language which appear to warrant the addition of extra consonant positions in the onset and the coda, apparently creating the new syllable types: CCV and CVCC. Words such as [na̲:.hni.ru] 'a while back', [he:.hla.thawa] 'he is hungry', and [si:.hru] 'house', appear to have CCV syllables on the surface.[6] It can be seen in the following examples, however, that these special /hC/ sequences within the same syllable are created only by the process of resyllabification, where two consonants associate to one skeletal position in the onset. (Some phonetic details have been omitted from these forms, as well as subsequent forms, in order to avoid confusing the reader with irrelevant information.)

(5) /na̲h/ + /ni/ + /txu/ → /na̲.hni.ru/ → [na̲:.Ni.ru]
  'a while back'
  /heh/ + /latha/ + /wa/ → /he.hla.tha.wa/ → [he:.La.tha.wa]
  'he is hungry'
  /sih/ + /txu/ → /si.hru/ → [si:.Ru]
  'a house'

Thus, we have separate segments from separate morphemes functioning as single consonants when they are juxtaposed. The /hn/ becomes the voiceless nasal [N], /hl/ becomes the voiceless lateral [L], and /hr/ is realized as an aspirated flap [R]. (The liquid flap, [r], is itself only an allophone of the phoneme /t/ in Mamaindé, but both [r] and [R] are used throughout this volume for phonetic transcriptions of an underlying /t/.) The following diagram shows how these apparent consonant clusters should be understood:

---

[6]Throughout this paper, any nonsurface form at any level is enclosed in slant lines (/ /), and the phonetic surface forms in brackets ([ ]).

(6) /hC/ clusters

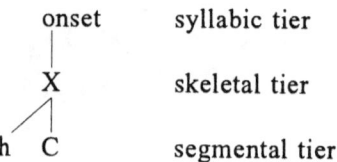

    onset   syllabic tier

    X   skeletal tier

   h C   segmental tier

Evidence that these /hC/ sequences are filling a single skeletal position comes from the fact that consonant clusters (which do not include pre- and postglottalized consonants) never occur in the onset of a Mamaindé syllable unless they are the result of the juxtaposition of two morphemes and the subsequent process of resyllabification. This argues against positing an additional syllable type, the CCV syllable, just to deal with these infrequent cases. It seems wiser to assume that this marked or uncommon syllable type will conform to the unmarked form ((C)V(X)) by associating the two adjacent consonant segments to a single onset position. Specific rules which describe this process of double association are discussed in upcoming sections. For now, note that by looking at these /hC/ sequences in this way, the result is to simplify the overall phonology and allow one to maintain the generalizations made earlier regarding the structure of the Mamaindé syllable.

This phenomenon of two consonants associating to one onset position occurs also in contracted forms, when syllables are juxtaposed by the deletion of intervening material. This is the only time the two sequences, [tʰw] and [kw], are found (/tʰ/ itself is a digraph of a single phoneme). Examples of this contraction process can be found in the forms below:

(7)   /na/+/la.tʰa/+/wa/   →   [na.la.tʰwa]   'he said'
      /tu/+/tax/+/wa/+/takxu/ → [tu.kwa:.ta.kxu] 'get and come'

A final type of consonant cluster that must be mentioned is the set of prestopped nasals. These are [gn], [bm], and [dn]. Prestopped nasals occur only in the coda position, and only when a syllable final /n/ is followed by a stop in the next syllable.

(8)   /yun/ + /txu/ → [yudn.du]   'knife'
      /wan.ka/   → [wagn.ka]   'to return'
      /waun + pa/   → [waubmba]   'to be two circles'

Because the prestopped nasals occur only as surface forms of a single underlying /n/, I propose that these phonetic consonant clusters in reality fill a single coda position in the phonology.[7]

Likewise, all diphthongs fill only one vowel position and not two. This means that diphthongs do not in themselves cause a syllable to be treated as heavy in Mamaindé phonology; it is only when they are followed by a coda element (either in the form of a coda consonant or extra length on the diphthong itself) that they become heavy syllables.

The previous discussion serves simply to point out that every Mamaindé syllable can be viewed as a subtype of a (C)V(X) structure, as diagrammed in (1).

2.2. Syllable weight. The distinction between light and heavy syllables is an important one throughout this paper. Current metrical theory defines a HEAVY syllable as one which has a branching rhyme, meaning that it contains both a nucleus and a coda. LIGHT syllables, on the other hand, do not have a branching rhyme, and therefore do not contain codas. The purpose of this distinction is to define precisely a phenomenon long noted in many languages, namely, that there are certain syllables which attract stress based on their internal structure. Goldsmith (1990) refers to this as the OBLIGATORY BRANCHINGNESS PRINCIPLE. Syllables with branching rhymes are obligatorily heavy. The converse also holds true, namely, that light syllables do not branch. Languages making use of this phenomenon, where heavy syllables attract stress, are known as QUANTITY-SENSITIVE languages. Those that do not have been characterized as QUANTITY-INSENSITIVE. A unique example of a language which defines syllable weight in a different way is Yupik, where apparently it is the branching nucleus, and not the rhyme, that constitutes a heavy syllable and attracts the most stress. (See Anderson 1984.)

Another way to look at the distinction between light and heavy syllables is to use the common term MORA. A mora is normally understood to mean "a minimal unit of metrical time equivalent to a short syllable" (Crystal 1985:198). Since both CV and V syllables are considered to be short in most languages, their mora value is actually the same; they are both only one mora in length. It is obviously only the nucleus, then,

---

[7]The actual point of articulation of these stops is usually predictable, as shown above. However, there are certain environments where these prestopped nasals do not follow natural assimilation rules. Further details of this rather complicated issue are beyond the scope of this paper; see Eberhard 1993.

which is being counted as a mora in these syllables, demonstrating the irrelevance of the onset position when calculating syllable weight.[8]

A syllable with a coda, however, is considered long in many languages, leaving us to deduce that such syllables are two mora in length, with the nucleus and the coda being equivalent to one mora each. Since most languages seem to make only a binary distinction between short and long syllables (Goldsmith 1990), regardless of the amount of material in the coda, we can assume that most syllables will be either one or two mora in length, and never any more.[9] This means that additional coda material, such as we find in a CVCC syllable, will not affect the metrical timing of that syllable, which will still be only two mora in length.[10] Thus, in most all cases, and for the purposes of this volume, light syllables will be only one mora in length, while heavy syllables are required to have a length of two mora. This basically means that in quantity-sensitive languages, the length of a coda is usually equivalent to the length of the onset and nucleus combined.

There is some interesting evidence in Mamaindé to support the existence of super-heavy syllables. Primary stressed syllables (indicated by ") with consonant codas seem to exaggerate the length of the coda, holding on to the unreleased consonant for what appears to be another mora in length, apparently creating a three-mora syllable.[11] For example:

(9) /"khatx/ + /txu/ → ["khatx:.txu] 'a stick'
     /"hãn/ + /takxu/ → ["hãn:.ta.kxu] 'to be white'

However, the stress system still seems to recognize only a binary distinction in syllable weight, since that is all that is necessary to account for stress placement. This extra coda lengthening, then, may just be an attempt by the language to emphasize that a specific syllable is

---

[8]Apparently there is at least one language, Mura-Pirahã, in which the presence and voicing of the onset must also be considered in determining the weight of a given syllable. See Everett 1986 for an interesting twist on the notion of quantity sensitivity.

[9]Of course, there appear to be exceptions here as well. In Estonian we find a ternary distinction between short, long, and overlong syllables (Goldsmith 1990). Southern Tepehuan also must distinguish between light, intermediate, and heavy syllables in its application of stress (Willett 1982).

[10]Word-final appendix material in some languages, however, must be considered as adding an extra mora beyond the coda of the final syllable. See Goldsmith 1990:202 for an introductory discussion of Arabic.

[11]Southern Nambiquára, one of the only two languages related to Mamaindé, also manifests this additional lengthening of coda consonants (Kroeker 1976).

The Mamaindé Syllable

heavy. If this is in fact just a phonetic alteration, a postlexical rule could easily account for this phenomenon. Such a rule might look something like the one in (10).

(10) Coda lengthening rule

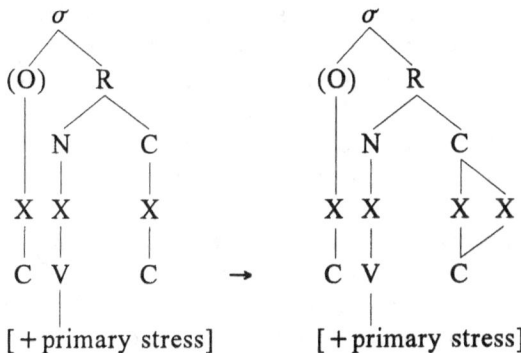

Basically, this rule states that whenever there is a primary stressed syllable (which, as I will show, can be formally characterized in a vertical grid) with a coda position filled, then an extra skeletal position is added to the coda, and the single coda segment associates to both of these positions, thus effectively lengthening the consonant. Since licensing theory predicts that licensers may license only one occurrence of any particular feature, the coda licenser in Mamaindé should license only one mora. This is exactly what appears to be happening, for this additional coda length does not add any extra level of stress to the syllable. As will be seen later, Mamaindé stress can be captured in a bi-moraic system, thereby making a three-mora system unnecessary. The extra skeletal position, then, is simply a phonetic lengthening of the coda which does not affect stress or syllable weight in any way.

In fact, since this lengthening occurs only on primary stressed syllables, all the stress rules must have already applied at the time the lengthening takes place. This rule would then be a part of the postlexical component, which is described in chapter 7 on lexical phonology. It also must precede the prestopped nasal rule (alluded to above but unfortunately beyond the scope of this paper); it is the coda lengthening rule that creates the necessary skeletal structure to which the prestopped nasal (and the so-called "syllabic" nasal) in Mamaindé may associate, allowing for a complex coda on the surface which is in reality only one nasal segment underlyingly. This coda lengthening rule, then, describes a widespread phenomenon in the language, and is discussed further in the section on lexical rules in chapter 8. This issue, however, is not yet completely resolved.

One unanswered question here is whether or not this coda lengthening rule adds any extra length to vowels which have already been lengthened, in other words, vowels which have already spread to an empty coda position via the vowel lengthening 1 (VL-1) rule (cf. (28)). There is some evidence in the language that when syllables without codas receive primary stress, the extra length on the vowel can appear to be more than just one mora in length. If this is so, the rule in (10) will have to be broadened slightly to allow for vowels in the coda position as well. For the present, though, the original rule is assumed.

2.3. Licensing theory. I borrow the idea of LICENSING from Goldsmith (1990) in order to better explain the co-restrictions found within the Mamaindé syllable. Licensing is a notion which follows logically from the widely held position that language structure is hierarchical and not simply linear. Syllables are not merely a sequence of unrelated segments, but in fact (as illustrated above) these segments are organized into higher levels of structure, such as onset, nucleus, and coda. The nucleus and coda can also be organized into a still higher level, the rhyme, and above that the syllable level. (Of course, this idea of hierarchy goes on to organize syllables into feet, feet into words, and so forth, all the way up through the phonological discourse level.)

If we accept the idea of hierarchy within language, then it is a simple matter to see how some higher levels could govern, or license, any material present on a lower level of structure. Goldsmith (1990:108) claims that

> all segments must be part of a higher-level organization, such as the syllable; each segment is licensed...by being a part of a larger unit, referring to the general condition as prosodic licensing.

But Goldsmith takes this idea still further. He claims that prosodic units license not only segments, but autosegments as well.[12] Goldsmith's crucial idea of autosegmental licensing claims that there are three

---

[12] I will assume the theory of autosegmental phonology is well known and will provide in this volume only those details of the theory which are particularly insightful as regards Mamaindé phonology. It will be noted that a hierarchical arrangement of autosegments (Clements 1985) with the explicit recognition of a laryngeal tier, a place tier, and a manner tier (these latter two combined into a supralaryngeal tier), finds support in this treatment.

prosodic units which have been "endowed by the grammar of the language with the ability to license a set of phonological features or, more precisely, autosegments" (Goldsmith 1990:123). These three units are: the SYLLABLE (the primary licenser), the CODA, and the APPENDIX (both secondary licensers). The syllable position is said to dominate both the onset and the nucleus positions and is always known as the primary licenser because it must license all of the distinctive features of a language (or only the contrastive features if underspecification is assumed, see discussion below). This comes from the fact that in every language all of the distinctive features utilized by the language can be found in either the onset or the nucleus, but none of these features will occur in both of these positions within a given string. Thus the onset and nucleus make up a single domain with respect to licensing by the syllable node. Codas and appendices (special word-final segments that cannot be syllabified in the coda), on the other hand, often restrict their licensing to a set of features which is a subset of those licensed by the syllable. In other words, codas and appendices normally impose more restrictions on segments than do the onset or nucleus. It is proposed that every autosegment must be licensed by one of the three licensing positions, and conversely, that each licenser may license only one occurrence of a particular autosegment.

Goldsmith ties this idea of licensing in with underspecification theory, which claims essentially that every distinctive feature utilized in a language must have a default, or unmarked setting. Only the marked value of a given feature is specified contrastively with the unmarked values added by redundancy rules. The phonology of a given language can thus be greatly simplified by removing all the unmarked features, which then eliminates all the redundancies and leaves only the contrastive ones. Segments which do not have the marked value of a given feature will not have any specification for that feature until that point in the phonology at which the unmarked values are filled in by the redundancy rules. Obviously, then, phonology rules cannot refer to the unmarked values of phonological features until these values are fully specified. Goldsmith proposes that this holds true also for licensing, so that syllabic structure may license only the contrastive or marked feature values of a language; unmarked values are not available for licensing.

While this combining of syllabic licensing and underspecification theory can make some powerful predictions across languages, I do not attempt to use underspecification theory in this paper. This is partly because the unmarked values of all the distinctive features in Mamaindé have not been definitively determined as yet, and partly due to the fact that in this paper I wish to focus on Mamaindé stress, something which can be done more efficiently and clearly without considering all the details of every phonological feature of the language. Thus, my use of Goldsmith's idea of licensing will be limited to the notion of syllabic restrictions on segmental material, without any underspecification assumed. By allowing full specification of all features in the phonology, it is possible to see, perhaps in a more explicit way, how this syllabic licensing works, and how these restrictions apply in this language.

2.4–2.6 Licensing in Mamaindé

2.4. The primary licenser. In Mamaindé, the syllable node licenses all the distinctive features of every Mamaindé phoneme (recall that the notion of underspecification is not being used here).

(11) Mamaindé Phonemes

Consonants

labial	alveolar	velar	glottal
p ph	t th	k kh	x (glottal stop)
	s		h
	l		
m	n		
w	y		

Vowels

i	u	a^i, i^u, a^u, e^u
e	o	
a		

In addition to this consonantal inventory, there is also a matching set of pre- and postglottalized counterparts for every consonant listed above. Since they occur in contrastive environments, they are viewed as separate phonemes (recall that they occur in the onset position, where there is no evidence that clusters occur). The glottalized imploded stops [$d^ʕ$] and [$b^ʕ$], however, are simply phonetic allophones of the /t/ and /p/ phonemes respectively.

Each vowel has a contrastive laryngealized or creaky voice counterpart, written with an underline (e.g., a̱), which is in contrast with the nonlaryngealized vowels. These are treated as vowels which are pre-associated to the feature [+constricted] on the laryngeal tier. In addition, each vowel also has nasalized counterparts, which can be viewed in almost all cases as predictable variants of underlying oral vowels. Although this analysis is not totally without problems, the nasalized vowels are not included in the set of Mamaindé phonemes (the reader is referred to a discussion on this phenomenon in Eberhard 1993).

Thus, we can have any of these phonological segments present in one or the other of the first two syllable positions, namely the onset and the nucleus. Practically speaking, of course, this means that the onset position can be filled by any single Mamaindé consonant: /h k l m n p s t w x y/ and any pre- or postglottalized version of these, which function as one segment; and the nucleus can be filled by any single vowel: /i u e o a a^i e^u a^u i^u/ and any laryngealized counterpart.[13]

2.5. The secondary licenser—coda. The coda position in Mamaindé licenses only the [−cont] feature on the manner of articulation tier. Only those segments which are full oral stops are allowed to occur in this position at the surface level (nasal stops are also considered to include a full oral stop). Specifically, /l s y w h/ do not occur. By using overt or positive specification of each distinctive feature, we will see that none of these segments can be considered [−cont], and therefore they are not licensed at this position.

Of those which do not occur in the coda in the output of the phonology, /h/ is the most interesting because it results in some dramatic examples of Mamaindé licensing. Word medially, /h/ always becomes resyllabified as an onset to the next syllable since it is not licensed by the coda. This behavior would actually be expected when the following onset was absent, due to the common (but not universal) process known as the MAXIMAL ONSET PRINCIPLE (Goldsmith 1990), where any intervocalic consonant is generally syllabified with a following vowel instead of with the preceding vowel (this process in Mamaindé is discussed in detail in §2.8). The /h/ in a Mamaindé coda, however, does resyllabify to the next onset position even when the onset is already occupied.

---

[13]This list of Mamaindé phonemes parallels the list found in Kingston (1976) with the exception of the [kw] and [khw] segments, which are present on his list but which I have not yet found necessary to include. The only recorded instances of these that I am aware of are the result of a contraction rule. The reader is also reminded that the vowel dipthongs will be viewed as single segments.

(12) Examples of syllable-final /h/

with no following onset:
sih + anxi → si:.ha.nxi 'the house'

with following onset:
sih + txu → si:.hru 'a house'

This interesting behavior of /h/ shows the force of the licensing restrictions in this language. Although many morphemes in the lexicon (such as /sih/ 'house') have /h/ in what looks like a coda position, in reality syllable structure has not been imposed on the morpheme in its lexical form. But as soon as the morpheme enters the phonology of the language, and the syllabification rule attempts to syllabify the string, the coda licenser does not accept the /h/ as a suitable segment since it is not [−cont]. This segment is then forced to associate to a position which licenses [+cont], namely, to the following onset if it is word medial, or to the appendix if it is word final. Notice in example (12) that the vowel preceding the /h/ also becomes lengthened, a detail which becomes important when we consider stress placement discussed below. This association of /h/ can be represented formally as follows in (13).

(13) Word medial resyllabification of /h/[14]

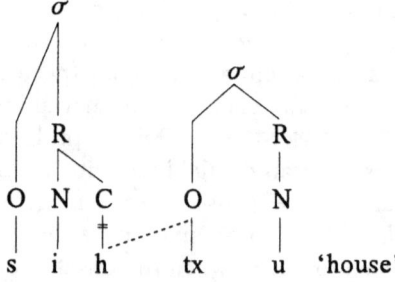

Note that the result of this association is a sequence of /htx/ assigned to a single consonant position. The word is pronounced [si:Ru], where [R] is a preaspirated flap. This behavior of the /h/ segment has been

---

[14]Following standard representations within autosegmental theory, here and elsewhere, solid lines show the environment of a rule, dashed lines show the structural change, and lines that have been crossed out represent a disassociation between two elements.

documented by Kingston in several of his writings ("Mamaindé Syllables" p. 5, "Mamaindé Phonology" pp. 32–35), although he does not mention the structural motivation behind such phenomena. He makes the statement that "the /h/ has a marked tendency to change places" ("Some Notes on Mamaindé Morphology and Morphophonemics" p. 6) noting several examples where /h/ is resyllabified from the coda of one syllable into the existing onset of the next, and where the preceding vowel is lengthened.

In "Mamaindé Phonology" (p. 34), Kingston also notes an alternative strategy dealing with /h/. He cites examples where an epenthetic vowel has been inserted directly between a syllable final /h/ and the following consonant onset. (The features of this inserted vowel are borrowed or spread from the previous vowel.) This allows /h/ to be resyllabified as an independent onset forming a new syllable, not with an original nucleus, but with an epenthesized nucleus.

(14) Kingston's examples of the epenthetic vowel strategy

/mih/ + /takxu/ → [mi:.hi.ta.kxu] 'it is cloudy'
/kanah/ + /tatxu/ → [ka.na.ha.ta.txu] 'tomorrow'

Notice how the inserted vowel borrows its features from the vowel on its left, being realized as an [i] in the first example and an [a] in the second.

We have now seen two strategies for dealing with /h/ in the coda. The first associates the /h/ with the onset position of the following syllable, regardless of whether it is already filled or not. The second builds a completely new syllable to which the /h/ then associates. Note that either of these strategies can be used on identical forms as shown in (15).

(15) /mih/ + /takxu/ → [mi:.Ra.kxu] 'it is cloudy'
     /mih/ + /takxu/ → [mi:.hi.ta.kxu] 'it is cloudy'

It appears, then, that there are alternative choices that Mamaindé speakers have at their disposal to correctly syllabify /h/ in accordance with the syllabic constraints of the language.

Besides /h/, there are other [+cont] segments which appear in the coda of certain underlying forms, namely, /s/ and /l/. But, like /h/, they fail to remain in that position on the surface. The /s/ segment, for example, is found as a coda in morphemes such as /na.kxas/ 'to listen'. This form, however, is never found alone, for as a verb stem, it is a bound morpheme, and will always take suffixes. Of course, when this morpheme is followed by a syllable without onset, the maximal onset principle causes the /s/ to be resyllabified as the onset of the next syllable.

(16) /na.kxas/ + /ax.wa/ → [na.kxa:.sax.wa]   'I listen'

The interesting thing to note here, however, is that when this morpheme is followed by a syllable with an onset position already filled, then the /s/ drops out completely.

(17) /na.kxas/ + /ta.hin.wa/ → [na.kxa:.ta.hin.wa] 'listen! (imperative)'

Here again we see the [−cont] coda licensing being enforced, so that the [+cont] /s/ may not remain in its original position, nor is it able to associate to the following onset position. This is because of the phonetic nature of /s/. Whereas /h/ may coalesce with other consonants to form a single segment which fills a single onset position, /s/ is phonetically unable to coalesce with any consonant and therefore may not share an association to the onset.[15] Licensing theory then predicts that any segment which cannot be licensed by some unit of prosodic structure must eventually be deleted. And as seen in example (17) above, deletion is exactly what occurs in Mamaindé. A more graphic illustration of that same form in (18) shows what happens to unassociated segments by convention at the end of the phonology.

---

[15]If it is assumed that /h/ has only the laryngeal feature [+ spread glottis] and no supralaryngeal features, its ability to combine with other segments having supralaryngeal specification is not unexpected. The fact that /s/ lacks this ability would find possible account in that its supralaryngeal specification prevents its combining with an additional segment or segments which have possible contradictory supralaryngeal features.

The Mamaindé Syllable

(18) Deletion of /s/

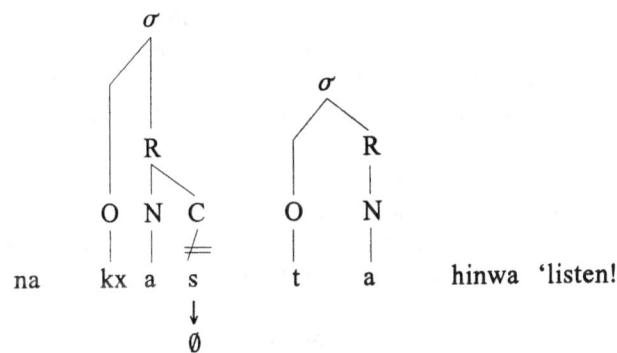

na kxas ta hinwa 'listen!'

According to Kingston, the /l/ segment has a similar fate in the coda position. He points out (personal communication) that any underlying /l/ in the coda of a Mamaindé syllable, when followed by /h/ in the onset of the next syllable, coalesces with the /h/ onset and becomes a voiceless lateral, represented here as [L], as in (19).

(19) /ãl/ 'indefinite agent' + /hãs.ka/ 'to turn white' →
[ã.Lã.ka] 'cause to turn white'

Notice how the [+cont] /l/ does not remain in the coda. Here it has been resyllabified as part of the onset of the next syllable. Followed by any other consonant, however, this coda /l/ is realized as [n] as shown in (20).

(20) /il/ 'house shaped thing' + /xau̯/ 'other' →
[in.xau̯] 'the other house'

Once again the /l/ has been prevented from occurring in coda position. Recall that [n] is considered a [−cont] segment and therefore does not violate the restrictions of the coda.

By understanding the notion of coda licensing, then, we can clearly see why the [+cont] segments in Mamaindé behave as they do.

2.6. The secondary licenser—appendix. The appendix licenses only those segments whose distinctive features include [+cont], [+spread glottis], or in other words, only /h/. Support for this claim can be found in that /h/ is the only segment which cannot appear at the end of a syllable unless that syllable happens to occur at the end of a word, such as /na-tʰoh/. This makes the Mamaindé /h/ a classic word-final appendix, a special position that exists only at the end of words. By positing that word final /h/ occupies an appendix position and not a syllable-coda position, we are able to keep the licensing restrictions we established for the coda, and thus maintain our generalization about the behavior of /h/. Otherwise we would be forced to say that /h/ usually does not appear in the coda even though word-finally it does. The presence of the appendix position removes such ambiguity.

As an appendix, /h/ is incorporated into the hierarchical structure only at the word level as shown in the diagram in (21).

(21) Word-final resyllabification of /h/[16]

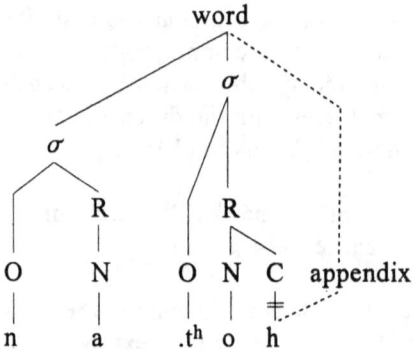

Kingston also notes that the strategy of inserting a vowel never occurs after a word-final /h/, which is expected since the word-final appendix position already licenses [+cont] and the extra vowel is consequently not needed. Again, this shows the ability of autosegmental licensing to capture natural restrictions within this language, and the ingenuity of the language in getting around them.

A final note about appendices. The Mamaindé appendix does not license an additional mora position on the metrical grid, although some other languages do allow this. This means that the Mamaindé appendix does not add any extra weight to the syllable in question, and thus can be considered extrasyllabic.

---

[16]Although /h/ never functions as a coda here, the presence of the coda position is crucial to the eventual lengthening of the preceding vowel, which spreads to the orphaned coda and thus retains the original weight of the syllable. See (29).

The Mamaindé Syllable

The previous discussion of the Mamaindé coda and appendix may seem a bit removed from the topic of stress. However, when we realize that these are the only syllable positions which could possibly affect the weight of a syllable, and when we recall that stress in Mamaindé is directly related to syllable weight, then it becomes important to be able to know with some degree of certainty whether a particular segment is syllabified as an onset, a coda, or an appendix.

2.7. The completed Mamaindé syllable. In the diagram in (22), the licensing elements have been added to the syllable structure diagram to complete the representation of the Mamaindé syllable.

(22) Mamaindé syllable structure (with licensing)

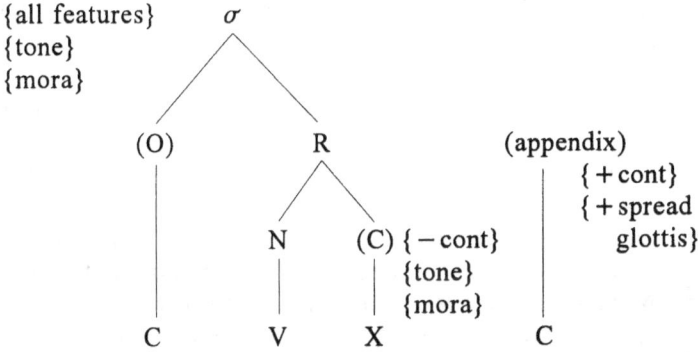

This diagram shows the addition of the autosegments of tone and mora to the licensing of both the syllable and the coda positions. Although tone is not treated in this paper, the tone autosegment is included here to show that tone is licensed by the same structures that license the mora, namely the syllable and the coda. This explains why Kingston noted that syllables with codas would always have two separate tones. This similar behavior of tone and mora seems to add additional support to the idea that the coda position is in fact a secondary licenser in Mamaindé.

Although [mora] is not usually treated as a feature, by including it here as an autosegment which is licensed by syllable structure, we can graphically show the quantity-sensitive nature of this language, where syllables can be one or two mora in length. This [mora] autosegment also gives us a formal basis upon which to build representations of stress in chapter 5, where [mora] can actually be regarded as the bottom row of these stress diagrams, known as METRICAL GRIDS. Thus to license [mora] is to license association to the mora-level row of the metrical grid. The diagrams in (23) (adopted from Goldsmith 1990:208) illustrate the different ways in which Mamaindé syllable structure may license a mora.

(23) Mora licensing in Mamaindé

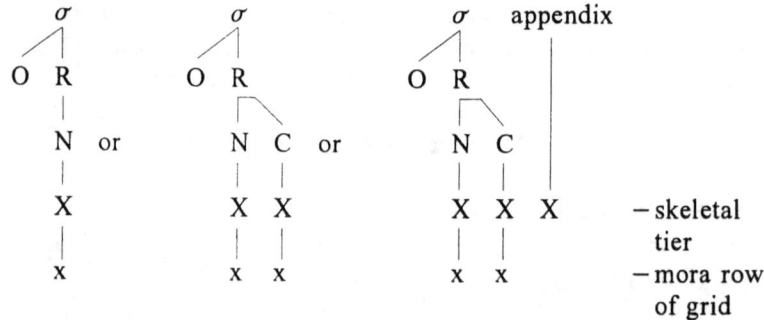

light syllable   heavy syllable   heavy syllable with appendix

Chapter 5 presents a detailed account of how the metrical grid can be constructed upon this first mora row to depict stress. At this juncture, however, Mamaindé stress is viewed simply as separate from, but autosegmentally associated to, syllable structure. (See Goldsmith 1990:193 for a discussion that supports the idea of metrical grids being viewed as autosegments.)

2.8. Syllabification. The task of syllabification in Mamaindé is an ongoing responsibility of the phonology. The initial syllabification process occurs automatically whenever a new morpheme enters the phonology. Although prosodic structure is not necessary in the underlying forms found in the lexicon, I propose that syllabification in Mamaindé occurs throughout the phonology, after every affixation process, building the largest possible syllables from left-to-right by applying the syllable structure diagrammed above in (22). Any segments which are not licensed by this structure are left unsyllabified. Those segments which are still unsyllabified after the last stage of the phonology are then deleted. Of course, what is most crucial to the task of syllabification is that the surface form output from the phonology be totally syllabified in accordance with the restrictions of the language.

The Mamaindé Syllable

This syllabification task includes two processes already mentioned: the maximal onset principle and vowel lengthening. Both of these involve a reevaluation of syllable structure, and the reassigning of the segmental string to the syllable.

As noted, the maximal onset principle applies in Mamaindé as it does in many languages. Thus any VC.V sequence becomes resyllabified as V.CV. This is demonstrated in the forms in (24).

(24) /hen/ + /a.nxi/ → /he:.na.nxi/ 'the time'
    /wet/ + /a.nxi/ → /we:.ta.nxi/ 'the child'
    /kax.yais/ + /ax/ + /wa/ → /kax.yai:.sax.wa/ 'I'm reading'
    /sun/ + /i/ + /txu/ → /su:.ni.txu/ 'a father-in-law'

Notice also the lengthening of the vowel in each of these examples. Because stress is quantity sensitive in Mamaindé, the same number of moras per syllable must be preserved after resyllabification occurs in order to maintain the original syllable weight and consequently to insure correct stress placement. I call this the PRESERVATION OF CODA PRINCIPLE. Both of these principles can be captured by the one simple formalism in (25).

(25) Maximal onset and preservation of coda

VC.V → V:.CV

The motivation behind these changes, however, can best be captured by two autosegmental rules which show that both the maximal onset principle and the preservation of coda principle are a result of autosegmental spreading (see (26) and (27)). In the first case, there is a reassociation of a consonant to a newly constructed onset, and in the second, the spreading of a vowel to an orphaned skeletal position.[17]

---

[17]Skeletal positions are simply sequential positions within the syllable which are filled by associating phonological material to them. They are not intended to represent mora. These skeletal positions are indicated in these representations by an upper case X.

(26) Environment of maximal onset principle, revised

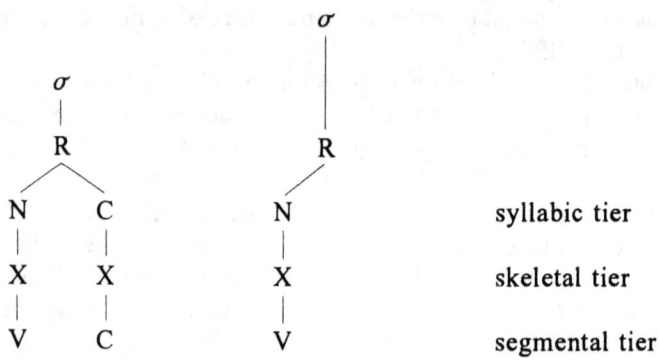

(27) Result of revised maximal onset principle

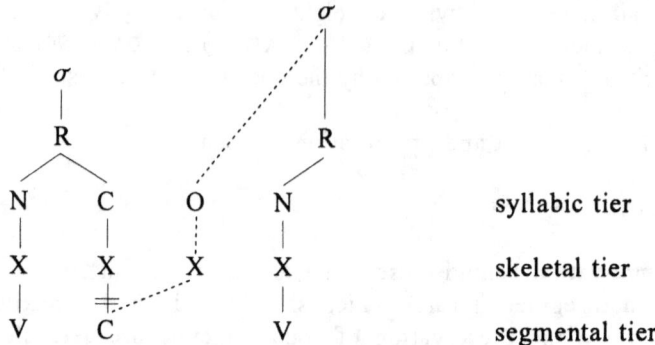

Notice how this rule constructs a new structural position, an onset, where there was none before, and then associates the coda segment to this new syllable position.

Consider now the rule in (28) which preserves the coda by lengthening the vowel.

The Mamaindé Syllable

(28) Vowel lengthening rule 1[18]

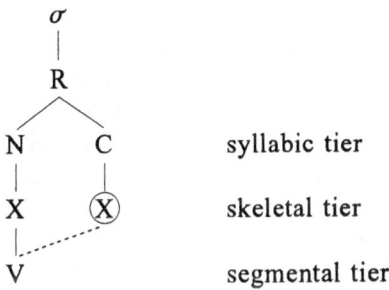

This rule spreads a vowel to an adjacent coda position which has previously been orphaned by the maximal onset principle, thus effectively lengthening the vowel. Obviously then there is a crucial relationship between the two rules such that it is the maximal onset principle whose application motivates application of the vowel lengthening rule in Mamaindé.

These two autosegmental processes can now be collapsed into one in (29) to show how they both apply to the same environment.

(29) Maximal onset principle and preservation of coda

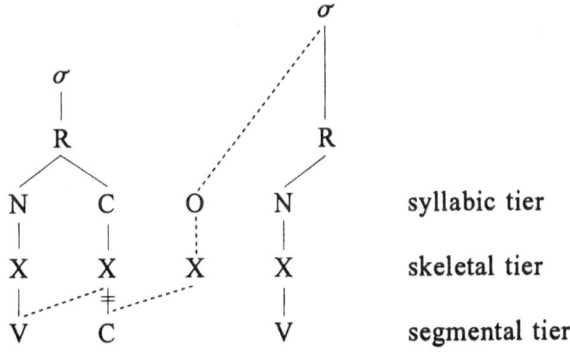

These cases are insightful examples of the naturalness of autosegmental spreading. Note that a coda does not need to be built in the first syllable to license the extra length of the vowel because a coda position

---

[18]Following tradition within autosegmental theory, a circle around a skeletal position shows that it has previously been "orphaned," or disassociated from the segmental tier, or otherwise unassociated.

already exists. Further, the spreading of the vowel segment is done naturally by vowel lengthening rule 1, where the orphaned skeletal position can be seen as the logical target for such a spreading rule.

What could be the formal motivation for such processes? Goldsmith (1990) mentions that the process of syllabification cross-linguistically has two common motivations: (1) To construct the fewest possible syllables within a given string (by building the largest syllables possible, either from right-to-left or left-to-right), and (2) To construct the fewest possible licensers.

In Mamaindé, both of these universal strategies are operative during syllabification. However, the second motivation creates only a temporary situation. The idea of constructing fewer licensers is the initial reason for the maximization of onsets. Since every coda adds another licenser, but onsets do not, consonant segments prefer to fill an onset as opposed to a coda position whenever possible in order to reduce the number of licensers. But, in the long run, the number of licensers is rarely changed in Mamaindé because of the vowel lengthening rule 1 which follows the maximal onset principle, and immediately fills any orphaned coda position with the previous vowel. This indicates that the need to maintain quantity sensitivity in this language is greater than the need to reduce licensers.

A summary of these rules showing their order and how they relate to the stress rules, is given at the end of chapter 8.

3
The Data and the Problem

3.1. The phonetics of Mamaindé stress. Before proceeding any further, it is necessary to determine what exactly is meant by stress. In this paper, stress is defined as a phonetic feature which gives a syllable prominence in relation to other syllables in a given string or utterance. How this prominence is encoded seems to vary across languages. Many languages use higher pitch to mark a stressed syllable. Others use greater intensity. Some use increased length. The majority seem to employ a combination of these phonetic options.

Although Mamaindé is a tonal language, the role of pitch does not function as a signal of stress. Stress may occur on any one of the four tones in the language (Kingston's tone numbers are used here: 1 falling tone, 2 rising tone, 3 low tone, 4 high tone, and one or more stress marks (") before a syllable for stress.).

(30) ha^3"yo:^{4} 'yes'
     "on^3ka^4 'work, do'
     ya^3"$l\underline{a}ux^1txu^3$ 'bracelet'
     wa^4"$nũn^2la^3tha^3wa^3$ 'it is good'

As can be seen in (30), the pitch of a syllable is not what gives it phonetic prominence in the word, although stress may in fact raise the phonetic pitch trajectory of each tone slightly. Stress, then, must be realized in another way.

One of the most obvious features of a stressed syllable in Mamaindé is its length, which has already been touched on. Notice the four words in (30). Every stressed syllable in this language appears to be heavy, having a length of two mora. Could length, then, be the phonetic "stuff" of Mamaindé stress? Although this is a tempting position to take, there are many heavy syllables which are not stressed. Notice the penultimate syllable in each of the words in (31).

(31) ["wa.ta.hin.wa]   'to come in'
     [i.ka."la.ka.nax.wa] 'I work'

Although these penultimate syllables are long, they are not stressed. There are also a few forms where the stressed syllable is not lengthened, such as the one in (32).

(32) [na.'la.tha.wa]   'it is'

For these reasons I assume that stress and length are not the same thing, although they are intricately tied together in this language, as is seen in §3.7.

The last phonetic variable to consider is intensity. All the stressed syllables in Mamaindé display an increased intensity in relation to those around them. This seems to be the only constant which is a dependable marker of stress. For the purposes of this study, then, stress in Mamaindé will be seen as a phonetic marking on certain syllables which increases their relative intensity. The question of how to predict this increased intensity is the subject of the remainder of this paper.

3.2. Basis of stress. The basic problem addressed in this study is how to predict stress in Mamaindé. Goldsmith (1990:114) mentions that there are three main ways in which languages assign stress: (1) On the basis of morphology, (2) On the basis of syllable location in the word, and (3) On the basis of internal syllable structure.

Many languages use only one of the above strategies. The most common ones seem to be the second or third. There are also a good number of languages which make use of these two simultaneously.[19] However,

---

[19] English stress has been analyzed by Goldsmith (1990) as having all three of the above strategies since it must appeal to word classes, using different extrametrical rules for nouns and verbs. He argues, however, that it does not require lexical strata for the stress rules to work, a notion which is shown later in this paper to be necessary in Mamaindé.

The Data and the Problem

as shown in the following chapters, in Mamaindé it is not possible to predict correct stress placement by using any one or two of Goldsmith's methods. The distinctive hypothesis presented in this paper is that Mamaindé requires the use of all three of these criteria, applied in a STRATAL approach, in order to account for stress.

3.3. The data. The word list in (33) gives a sampling of Mamaindé data with stress indicated as follows: one stress mark (') for secondary stress, two (") for primary stress, and three (''') for emphatic stress.

(33) Mamaindé data

'sux."ton.ta.la.tha.wa   'it isn't known to me'
'set."ten.la.tha.wa   'he will speak'
"set.'''yex.'let.nan.wa   'he surely did speak'
ha."yo: 'yes'
'i.ka."la:.ka.la.tha.wa   'he is working for'
'i.ka."la:."kuh.'tex.na.'tax 'in order to work with'
wa.le."khan.txu   'chief'
ha."lo:.txu   'land'
ma."main.si.a.nxi   'the cared-for ones—the Mamaindé'
"su:.ni.txu   'father-in-law'
"wa:."hen.i.'yah.a.nxi   'the exact time of coming'
'hax."tin   'quickly'
"eu:.'tex.na.'tax   'in order to see'
wa.'sen.na."sa:.txu   'your spoken speech'
'kax."yais.ax.wa   'I am writing'
yu."hakx   'all'
'kax."yaix.'let.nan.wa   'he wrote'
'sux."ton.ta.'let.nan.wa   'I did not know'
"on.ka.kha.'tox   'work, then'
"wa:.nun.ta.wa   'you obviously will come'
wa."nũn.ax.wa   'I am good'
"tu:.ta.kxu   'get'
tu."wa:.ta.kxu   'get and come, bring'
ta."wet.txu   'my child'
'ta.ha."lo:.txu   'my land'
"xai:.'tex   'in order to go'
na.'la.tha.wa   'it is'

A quick glance at the above data provides some basic information. First of all, the Mamaindé stress system has at least three phonetic levels of stress; secondary ('), primary ("), and emphatic ('"), listed from weakest to strongest. (See chapter 4 for a more detailed discussion of stress levels.) All three of these stress levels are evident on the form in (34).

(34) "set.'"yex.'let.nan.wa   'he surely did speak'

Another fact is that this is a QUANTITY-SENSITIVE language, where heavy syllables consistently attract some degree of stress. Heavy syllables, as we noted in the first chapter, are those which contain coda material. Light syllables do not. In Mamaindé, this coda position can be filled with either a consonant, or the extra length of a long vowel. Notice that throughout the data given here, heavy syllables consistently receive stress in almost any position within the word (there are some important exceptions to this which will be discussed shortly):

(35) "wa:."hen.i.'yah.a.nxi   'the exact time of coming'

3.4–3.7 The Problem

A closer look at the data reveals a problem as yet unhandled. The notion of quantity sensitivity, appealing to the internal make-up of the syllable, does not account for all the stress patterns in the data above. Neither does there seem to be any favored syllable position. How, then, can stress placement be predicted in this language? There are four individual problems to be addressed.

3.4. Problem 1. Unpredictable word-level stress. The first problem is that there seems to be no way to determine which heavy syllables receive primary stress and which receive secondary stress. Neither the secondary nor the primary stresses seem to make any reference to the notion of syllable or foot position within the whole word. Even in quantity-sensitive languages, where secondary stress is determined by syllable weight, primary stress normally must choose one of the available feet on the basis of its position within the word. Generative phonology has many terms to describe this relative positioning, including such notions as left- or right-headedness, perfect grid, end rule final, and end rule initial (these are discussed in detail in chapter 5). There are two observations which have consistently held true for many languages: (1)

The Data and the Problem

The position of stressed syllables in a given language should normally be predictable (within the foot or word), and (2) The position of these stressed syllables should be peripheral (within that larger unit).

This means that, if Mamaindé is similar to most languages, the stress should be consistent. It also means that this stress should always be on the right or left margin of a particular domain, and not in the middle (ignoring for a moment such things as extrametrical material, which is discussed later).

As the data show, however, Mamaindé appears to contradict both of these observations. From the surface there seems to be no favored position for stress. At times, primary stress can be found at the LEFT EDGE of words (and BEFORE secondary stress) as in (36).

(36) "x<u>a</u>i.xna.'ten.ax.wa   'I will go'

Although the boundaries of feet in Mamaindé have not yet been defined, it can safely be assumed that the word in (36) has at least two feet (one for every stress), and that the primary stress falls on the left-most foot.

At other times primary stress is located on the RIGHT EDGE of the word (and AFTER secondary stress) as in (37).

(37) 'hax"tin   'quickly'

Therefore such a word has two feet, with the primary stress falling on the right-most foot.

However, primary stress can even occur in the MIDDLE of the word, BETWEEN two secondary stressed syllables, as opposed to being located on either extremity of the string; see (38).

(38) 'kax."yaix.'let.nan.wa   'he wrote'

This forces us to conclude that some words have at least three feet with primary stress falling on the middle foot, instead of on a marginal foot as current theory would suggest.

There are also words which have more than one primary stressed syllable as shown in (39):

(39) "w<u>a</u>:."hen.i.'yah.a.nxi   'the exact time of coming'

All of these cases seem to imply that the placement of primary stress in this language is arbitrary from the perspective of the whole word.

3.5. Problem 2. Unstressed heavy syllables. Secondly, although it clearly appears to be a quantity-sensitive language, Mamaindé has some heavy syllables which do not attract stress at all (notice *ax* in the first example of (40) and *nun* in the second).

(40) *wa."nũn.ax.wa*   'I am good'
      "wa:.nun.ta.wa   'you obviously will come'

These unstressed heavy syllables cause a grave problem for a quantity-sensitive hypothesis, a problem which must be resolved. To further complicate things, these syllables are not located at word boundaries, and thus cannot be explained in terms of the common notion of extrametricality, which is discussed in chapter 5.

3.6. Problem 3. Light syllables which receive stress. The data also reveal some secondary stressed syllables which are not heavy, such as the words in (41).

(41) *'ta.ha."lo:.txu*   'my land'
      na.'la.tha.wa   'it is'

How these light syllables came to be stressed is a further question that needs to be answered in any analysis of Mamaindé stress.

3.7. Problem 4. Lengthened vowels in underlying forms. The last problem deals with lengthened vowels. The data give us some reason to believe that vowels are all short in their underlying form. Consider the two forms in (42).

(42) *"tu:.ta.kxu*   'getting'
      tu."wa:.ta.kxu   'to get and come, bringing'

The first word has only one root morpheme, /tu/ 'get'. The second word contains a compound root, /tu/ 'get' and /wa/ 'come' which together connote 'bring'. Notice that the root morpheme /tu/ contains a lengthened vowel in the first but not in the second example. This suggests that length is not actually a part of that morpheme but can be added to it by some rule. A later argument shows that this hypothesis is correct;

long vowels are never part of the underlying forms in this language. This fact greatly reduces the inventory of phonemes and simplifies the forms found in the lexicon. However, it also makes it necessary to have a rule to stress those syllables which are not originally heavy (as well as the rule which then lengthens them). By looking at the Mamaindé word as a whole, it is virtually impossible to create such a stress rule. This, then, is another problem which must be addressed.

Aside from the difficulty of predicting stress, these four problems also have theoretical ramifications. The first (§3.4) suggests a language in which metrical feet, and therefore stress, cannot be defined in terms of syllable position, such as right- or left-headedness. This in turn has a direct impact on the question of formalism within current metrical theory, i.e., can stress in all languages be equally defined by both the tree and grid approaches? The second problem mentioned above (§3.5) creates a difficulty when trying to apply the common theory of extrametricality to these forms. The last two problems (§§3.6–3.7) will eventually cause me to posit three secondary or foot-level stress rules for this language, something which is not at all common. All of these difficulties are discussed in more detail at appropriate points throughout this paper. For now, these crucial areas have been pointed out in order to show what problems must be dealt with by any acceptable analysis of Mamaindé stress.

3.8. Methodology. For the sake of understanding the discussion to follow, it might be helpful to consider three alternative approaches to the problems of Mamaindé stress, evaluating each approach, and pointing out its strengths and weaknesses. The third and final analysis presented in chapter 8 is the one which I believe provides the most adequate solution currently available.

The first approach to be considered is Kingston's analysis, which is based primarily on morphology. The second is a straightforward metrical analysis, based on syllable position and internal structure. The last approach shares all three stress-assigning strategies listed in §3.2 (morphology, syllable position, and syllable structure) but adds the crucial notion of strata as it is proposed in lexical phonology.

3.9. Theory power. How much power is needed? If the "powerfulness" of each approach were rated, the first one to be considered, Kingston's analysis in chapter 4, is by far the most powerful, with few restrictions on stress placement other than the grammatical class of each morpheme. The only specific stress rules provided by Kingston refer to morphology, as the understanding of Mamaindé's complex morphology was Kingston's main objective in analyzing stress. Other variations of stress not accounted for by morphology are apparently allowed to be a part of the speaker's memory bank.

In generative linguistics, however, it is preferable to discover, if possible, the smallest set of rules that will adequately explain a human language behavior, in this case, Mamaindé stress placement. Behind this goal lies the assumption that most language behavior is ordered and predictable. With this assumption as a premise, we will move from Kingston's "powerful" approach to the other extreme, in an attempt to find the simplest and "weakest" solution for the data. This is the metrical approach found in chapter 6. As is soon apparent, however, more power is actually required, and a move toward a less restricted lexical approach is discussed in chapter 8, with a final solution that is somewhere between the two extremes—sharing some of the restrictions of the metrical approach, but at the same time, requiring the more powerful reference to Kingston's morpheme classes.

4
A Previous Solution

4.1. Levels of stress. This chapter presents a look at the only other analysis ever done on Mamaindé stress. Peter Kingston, in an unpublished manuscript entitled "Mamaindé Syllables," specifies five levels of stress (in another paper, "Mamaindé Phonology," he actually lists six levels; although neither paper is dated, I believe the analysis referring to five levels represents his more recent analysis). His five rules are as follows:

Level 1. Secondary affix stress—assigned to all affixes which are not primary or root affixes.
Level 2. Primary affix stress—assigned to affixes which at times can function as roots.
Level 3. Root stress—assigned to all roots.
Level 4. Phrase stress—assigned to syllables found in certain locations in the phrase (to be detailed later).
Level 5. Inherent stress—reserved for specific emphatic and negative morphemes.

Although Kingston posits five levels of stress instead of the three that I have mentioned, there is not that much difference in actuality. His first level of stress, Level 1, corresponds (more or less) to the mora row in the metrical grid approach since it applies to all syllables. In metrical phonology, this mora row is not generally considered to constitute distinctive stress, but rather a basis for stress to build on. Therefore in metrical terms it is often referred to as "Level 0" (see chapter 5 for details). This, then, is simply a difference in terms.

The only real difference in the number of stresses that have been posited is that in the present paper I have chosen to ignore phrase-level stress (a phenomenon which seems to be linked to intonation in Mamaindé and is easily predictable), in order to focus on stress at the word level and below, where the real problem of characterizing stress is located. In other words, instead of dealing with the relative prominence of syllables across an entire phrase, I am concerned with their relative prominence within individual words. The reader can, however, find a description of Kingston's phrase-level stress rules under the post-lexical rules of chapter 8, §8.3.[20]

I will not spend much time discussing Kingston's INHERENT STRESS which is linked only to the emphatic morphemes, such as *yex,* and the negative morpheme *áx*. This inherent stress is, however, contrastive with other levels of stress within individual words and has the strongest prominence. It is found only on an extremely small subset of morphemes, however, whereas the foot- and word-level stresses are found in almost every word. More importantly, inherent stress is not affected by the rules which govern all other stresses within the language. It is simply connected to emphatic or negative morphemes regardless of their position within the word or phrase. I believe Kingston is correct in calling this "inherent stress," meaning that a small defined set of emphatic and negative morphemes is marked for the highest level of stress within the lexicon.

In autosegmental terms, these morphemes may be considered to be pre-associated to a [+phrase-level stress] autosegment before leaving the lexicon. In metrical grid terms, this stress autosegment could be represented as a set of grid marks depicting stress at different levels of metrical structure. Since the inherently stressed morphemes in Mamaindé always receive the highest level of stress over the domain of an entire phrase, they must be preassociated to a set of four grid marks,

---

[20]Actually, even Kingston's rules for phrase-level stress do not actually constitute a different level of phonetic prominence per se; they simply raise the stress of levels 1–3 to the next higher level depending on the intonation pattern of the phrase. This is done regardless of that syllable's initial stress level, unless it happens to be an emphatic morpheme which is already stressed to the highest level possible and thus cannot be raised any more.

A Previous Solution   37

one for each level of structure up through the phrase level. Thus the morpheme *yex* would be listed in the lexicon as shown in (43).[21]

(43)   x   phrase level
       x   word level
       x   foot level
       x   mora level
       |
      /yex/ 'emphatic morpheme'

As in the case of phrase-level stress, no further discussion of inherent stress is included here, but rather the focus is on the foot- and word-level stresses which are at the heart of Mamaindé phonology. I do believe, however, that the inherent stress of Mamaindé does merit its own study, particularly in regard to the negative construction, which is extremely interesting and complex within this language.

The chart in (44) presents the correspondences between Kingston's stress levels and the ones used in the present paper:

(44) Kingston   Present analysis

     Level 1   mora row (no stress)
     Level 2   foot level (secondary stress ')
     Level 3   word level (primary stress ")
     Level 4   phrase level
                 (is not indicated in my data since it appears mainly as
                 an intonational device over extended speech, a separate
                 topic which merits its own study)
     Level 5   inherent stress (emphatic and negative ''')

Throughout the remainder of this paper stress is marked according to the analysis above, which associates the relative prominence of each syllable to the hierarchical structure at which this prominence is evident, i.e., at the mora level, the foot level, or the word level.

4.2. Application of Kingston's stress rules. Notice how Kingston's rules listed above make crucial reference to the morphological category

---

[21]For more details on metrical grid theory, see chapter 5. Chapter 9 shows a complete derivation of a word containing one of these inherently stressed morphemes. In chapter 10 a discussion on viewing the metrical grid as an autosegment is included.

of each morpheme. Level 1 stress is for secondary affixes, level 2 is for primary affixes, level 3 is for roots, level 4 is for phrase stress, and level 5 is reserved for the inherently stressed morphemes. This appeal to morphology is the first strategy mentioned earlier as a means by which languages may apply stress. In Mamaindé this morphological strategy is an essential first step in unraveling its complex stress system. The different stress levels posited by Kingston can be observed on the following forms (all roots are in small caps, and stress levels are indicated by numbers above each syllable (Level 4 has been omitted in these examples since it occurs only at the phrase level in extended speech.)).

In (45) *set* is a root, *yex* is an emphatic morpheme, *let* is a primary affix, and the rest are secondary affixes.

(45) 3   5   2   1   1
      "SET- '"yex- 'let- nan- wa
      'he surely spoke'

In (46), *ta-* is a prefix (or secondary affix), *wet* is a root, and *-txu* is another secondary affix.

(46) 1   3   1
      ta- "WET- txu
      'my child'

In (47) *xai* is a root and *tex* is a primary affix.

(47) 3   2
      "X<u>A</u>I:. 'tex
      'in order to go'

The above forms are all accurate. By making reference to these morphological categories, Kingston is able to capture a great deal about stress in this language. However, there is more to this stress system than what can be accounted for by morphology alone.

4.3. Problems with the morphological stress rules. Unfortunately, the morphological stress rules are not totally adequate. Why do some morphemes which are in the same morphological category get stressed differently? Take, for example, the pair of words in (48).

A Previous Solution

(48) 2 1 3   1 1 1   1
    'i. KA. "LA:. ka. la. tha. wa
    'he is working for'

    2 1 3   3   2   1   2
    'i. KA. "LA:. "kuh. 'tex. na. 'tax
    'in order to work with'

The syllable immediately following the root in both of these words is a type of prepositional morpheme. In the first, -ka is the benefactive morpheme; in the second, -kuh is the comitative morpheme. Since they fulfill similar grammatical functions and are located in the same position in the word, we would expect them to belong to the same morpheme class. However, one receives level 1 stress (or no stress) and the other level 3 stress. Even more telling is when the very same morpheme receives different stress levels in different environments, as in the first-person-possessive prefix *ta-* in the examples in (49).

(49) 2   1   3   1
    'ta. HA. "LO:. txu
    'my land'

    1   3   1
    ta. "WET. txu
    'my child'

Another example of a morpheme which is not stressed according to its morphological category is the verb root *na-* 'to be, to say'. As a root it should be stressed to level 3, yet this root does not receive any stress. Note the examples in (50).

(50) 1   1   2
    NA- kha. 'tox
    'then'

    1   2   1   1
    NA- 'let- nan- wa
    'he said'

Another question that remains unanswered with a strictly morphological analysis is which syllable receives the stress if a given morpheme has more than one syllable? In (51) both the root, *tanu*, and the primary affix, *khatox*, have two syllables.

(51) 1   3   1   2
     TA. "NU. kha. 'tox
     'give, then'

How do we determine which syllable receives the regular stress for such morphemes? Obviously we must look beyond morphology.

Not only is it necessary to determine which syllable receives the stress in a polysyllabic morpheme, but also to be able to account for two different levels of stress on many polysyllabic roots. For example, the roots in (52) have more than one stress level and, again, morphology is of no help here.

(52) 2   3
     'SUX. "TON
     'to not know'

      2   3
     'KAX. "YAIS
     'to write'

      2   3
     'HAX. "TIN
     'quickly'

4.4. Quantity sensitivity. Kingston mentions in another section of his paper "Mamaindé Syllables," that all stressed syllables must be two moras in length, and all unstressed syllables one mora in length. This reference to quantity sensitivity, as noted in chapter 1, is a major key to Mamaindé stress. Yet Kingston never combined it in any way with the morphological stress rules. Therefore, there is no way to know which aspect of his stress system had priority in Kingston's analysis, the morphological stress rules or its quantity-sensitive nature. For example, when a secondary affix is composed of one heavy syllable, such as *nax* (second person subject), and the morphological stress rules do not assign it any stress (or, in other words, stress level 1), will quantity sensitivity apply and stress the heavy syllable anyway? When a primary affix is composed of one light syllable, such as *ta* 'to me', and the morphological stress rules assign it a level 2 stress, will the quantity-sensitive nature of

A Previous Solution

this language take over and prevent that light syllable from being stressed? These are unanswered questions in Kingston's analysis. Another important question which Kingston does not address relates to the lengthening of vowels within a quantity-sensitive system. Do these heavy syllables become stressed because they are heavy, or do they become heavy because they are stressed? Such basic questions must be answered before stress placement in this language can be predicted.

4.5. Syllable position. Although positing morphology as the basis for Mamaindé stress, Kingston ("Mamaindé Syllables," p. 2) does make mention of syllable position by saying that "the favored stress pattern is trochaic."[22] Yet Kingston also mentions that this trochaic pattern is often not possible. Note the trochaic examples in (53).

(53) Trochaic pattern (stressed and unstressed)

'i.ka."la:.ka.'tex.na.'tax   'in order to work'
'ta.ha."lo:.txu   'my land'
'nu.sa."wet.txu   'our child'
"wet.txu   'child'

Unfortunately, Kingston formulates no specific rules for this trochaic tendency. Does the trochaic stress pattern apply only to feet, or to words as well? Are these constituents constructed from left-to-right or from right-to-left? He also does not mention when this trochaic pattern of stress is favored or not favored, or if it is supposed to be active only in certain morphological categories. Although there are examples of trochaic patterns in Mamaindé, many times an opposite pattern emerges, known as iambic stress.[23] Note the examples in (54).

---

[22]Trochaic refers to an alternating stress pattern beginning with a stressed syllable, when going from left to right. In metrical theory such a pattern is characterized as manifesting binary left-headed feet, which are constructed from left to right. An example of a trochaic stress pattern is found in the English word 'ala'bama.

[23]Iambic feet produce an alternating stress pattern beginning with an unstressed syllable, when going from left to right. An example of an iambic foot pattern is found in the English word o'rangu'tang.

(54) Iambic pattern (unstressed and stressed)

    wa.'sen.na."sa:.txu   'your spoken speech'
    ta."nu:.kha.'tox   'give, then'
    ha."lo:.txu   'land'

Most frequently, however, there is no obvious pattern of stress at all in Mamaindé words as a whole. Consider the words in (55).

(55)   'sux."ton.ta.la.tha.wa   'it is not known to me'
    "set."ten.la.tha.wa   'he will speak'
    "set.'"yex.'let.nan.wa   'he surely did speak'
    'i.ka."la:."kuh.'tex.na.'tax   'in order to work with'
    wa.le."khan.txu   'chief'
    "wa:."hen.i.'yah.a.nxi   'the exact time of coming'

Because of the variety of stress patterns at the word level, no consistent rule can be posited for stress after the morphology has been built. But as we shall see, when we break words into their morpheme constituents, the pattern emerges.

First, it is necessary to study the root morphemes in isolation. Take the roots in the words in (56).

(56) prefix   root   suffix

prefix	root	suffix	
wa-	HA"LO	-txu	'your land'
ta-	YU"MĬ	-txu	'my nose'
	TA"WA	-nunxnalathawa	'he commanded'
	TA"NU	-tanaxwa	'you gave me'
	KHE"KHE	-takxu	'to walk slowly'
i-	KA"LA	-kuhtexnatax	'in order to work with'
nusa-	WALE"KHAN	-txu	'our chief'

In general terms, any polysyllabic root is stressed on the right-most syllable. This produces an iambic pattern in bisyllabic roots instead of a trochaic one. Even when both syllables of the root are equally heavy, as in the words in (57), and it would appear that nothing is hindering a trochaic stress pattern, the right-most syllable of the root still carries the heavier stress, keeping the root morpheme iambic.

A Previous Solution

(57) 'SUX."TON.   -ta.-la.tha.-wa   'it is not known to me'
      unknown   -to me-3pers-decl

      'KAX."YAIS   -ax-wa   'I am writing'
      write   -1p-decl

      'EN."KUN   -latha-wa   'he is healing'
      heal   -3pers-decl

      'HAX."TIN   'rapidly'
      rapidly

The question is why was a trochaic pattern posited in the first place? The problem here is that Mamaindé words, taken as whole units, often tend to have the highest levels of stress on the left end of the string, because there are relatively few prefixes compared to suffixes. This almost always leaves the higher stressed root towards the left of most words, thus appearing to be trochaic. But as noted above, there are many examples to the contrary.

In summary, I do not believe that a trochaic pattern is part of the basic Mamaindé stress rules, since all polysyllabic morphemes, taken in isolation, tend to be iambic rather than trochaic. This shows that there actually is a consistent stress rule in Mamaindé which refers to the position of the syllable. This position is the right-most syllable in the string. Exactly how this rule is formulated is spelled out in chapter 8. It is this crucial reference to right-headedness that was missing from this first approach to Mamaindé stress.

In all fairness, however, it is clear that Kingston's main emphasis was on the morphological basis of stress, and not on the relative position or weight of the syllables. At the beginning of his phonology, he states, "stress is normally predictable, when the grammatical function of each morpheme is taken into account" (Kingston, "Mamaindé Syllables," p. 2). Although there is much more that needs to be taken into account besides morphology, it becomes apparent in the final analysis that he was correct in appealing to the notion of morpheme class.

By using other approaches in following chapters, an attempt is made to answer the questions raised here.

5
An Overview of Metrical Phonology

The theory of metrical phonology[24] was initially developed by Liberman and Prince (1977). The basic foundation of this theory is that stress is best treated as the relative prominence between syllables (as opposed to a property of vowel quality). Metrical phonology then takes the next logical step and claims that this relative prominence between syllables is a result of the constituent structure of the words and phrases in question; in other words, stress is a direct product of the way in which consonants and vowels are built into syllables, syllables are built into feet, and feet into words.

The above premise has led to two different types of formalisms, the metrical tree and the metrical grid.

5.1. Arboreal theory. Originally, metrical trees were simply hierarchical structures with branches marked *s* for strong and *w* for weak; *F* represents the foot structure. Take the English word *Alabama* in (58).

---

[24]This chapter is based on Goldsmith's *Autosegmental and Metrical Phonology* 1990.

(58)

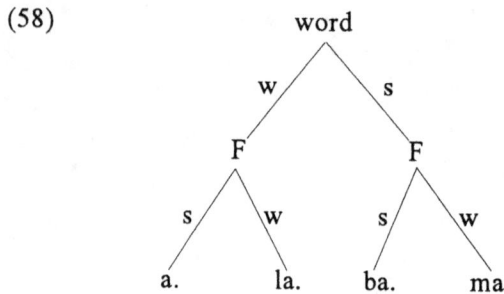

Later an alternate notation was introduced which was called head-marked notation, where the node representing the foot is placed vertically above the rhyme that is stressed, and the node representing the word is placed vertically above the foot that receives primary stress, which resulted in the tree in (59).

(59)

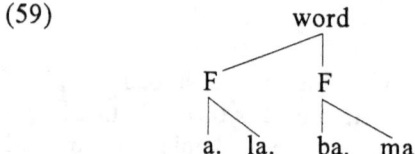

Metrical rules are proposed which build the structures necessary to account for the stress patterns in any language. One of the appealing aspects of this theory is that a remarkably small inventory of rules is needed to characterize the stress patterns of a large cross-section of the world's languages. There are basically only five parameters which must be set to predict stress in a given language (Goldsmith 1990). These are listed in (60).

(60) Parameters of arboreal theory

    Parameter 1: left or right-headed feet
    Parameter 2: bounded or unbounded feet
    Parameter 3: quantity sensitive or quantity insensitive
    Parameter 4: left-to-right or right-to-left application
    Parameter 5: suppression of secondary stress: yes/no

The first parameter states whether the feet of the language in question are stressed on the leftmost (left-headed) or rightmost (right-headed) syllable.

The second parameter states the maximum number of syllables allowed in a given foot. The tendency is either BINARY feet (which are considered bounded) or UNBOUNDED feet where any number of syllables is possible. (Mura-Pirahã, however, as Everett (1986) points out, is a language where ternary feet are required.)

The third determines whether or not the language attaches any significance to the internal structure of the syllable, particularly the rhyme, in its assignment of stress. We mentioned in chapter 1 that those languages which are quantity sensitive must have "obligatory branchingness" (Goldsmith 1990) within the rhymes of their stressed syllables. Simply stated, quantity-sensitive languages will always stress those syllables which have a coda position (whether consonant or vowel for most languages) whereas quantity-insensitive languages show no favoritism to such syllables.

The fourth indicates which end of the string one must start at in order to build the correct foot and word structures. This can be shown by the existence of DEGENERATE feet (feet which contain but a single syllable in a language with bounded feet) at one end or the other of a string; the degenerate foot will be at the left edge of the word if feet are built from right to left, and at the right edge if they are built from left to right.

The last parameter, suppression of secondary stress, is not really a stress rule but a language specific trait. Some languages actually have binary foot structures which are constructed but do not allow the stress of weak feet at the word level to be phonetically realized.

One other consideration to be made in applying metrical theory is the notion of EXTRAMETRICALITY. Although Goldsmith does not include this as one of the five parameters, he makes extensive use of this common principle in his analysis. An extrametrical syllable is one upon which a foot structure may not be constructed, and therefore it may never be stressed. In essence, it remains invisible to the rules which build constituent structure. Current theory holds that such extrametrical syllables must be peripheral, i.e., at one end or the other of the word. This is known as the PERIPHERALITY CONDITION (Harris 1982). Statements of extrametricality should also be expressible in simple generalizations by referring either to all words in the language or to definable word classes. For example, in English, one must mark the final syllable of nouns as extrametrical. This is indicated formally by putting parentheses around the syllable in question; for example, in the noun *elasticity*, the last syllable is marked as extrametrical in (61) and is consequently ignored by the rules which build the feet and word structures. (Extrametrical syllables are incorporated directly into the word-level structure by the principle of STRAY SYLLABLE ADJUNCTION.)

(61)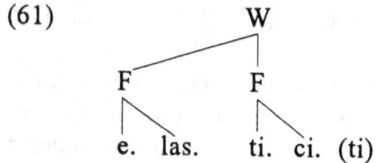

Having set these parameters, the construction of metrical structure is rather straightforward, first applying these parameters at the foot level and then at the word level. It is important to note, however, that parameters for these two levels are set independently and therefore may be different; actually, at the word-level, only the parameters of headedness and directionality are relevant. Also possible at the word level is the parameter of SUPPRESSION OF SECONDARY STRESS, for which the setting may be *yes* or *no*. If *yes*, then any foot which is not the head of the phonological word receives no stress. Finally we can arrive at a system which should be able to predict the stress of the language for which it was created.

For the English word *Alabama*, for example, the parameters would be set as shown in (62) resulting in the tree in (63). (This is just an example of how these parameters work and is in no way intended to represent actual English stress rules, which are far more complicated.)

(62) Parameters set at the foot level

Parameter 1: construct left-headed feet
Parameter 2: direction of application: not crucial
Parameter 3: quantity sensitive/insensitive: not crucial here
Parameter 4: bounded feet
Parameter 5: suppression of secondary stress: no
Extrametricality: none

(63)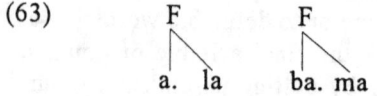

Then we would need to set the parameters for the word level as in (64) (where only the first two could actually apply):

An Overview of Metrical Phonology

(64) Parameter 1: construct right-headed words
Parameter 2: direction of application: not crucial
Parameter 5: suppression of secondary stress: no

This word structure is then built upon the previous foot structure to give us the completed arboreal tree in (65).

(65)

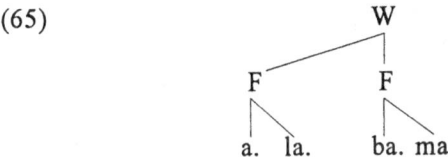

Notice that foot structure can be left-headed within a right-headed word and vice versa because the parameters for foot and word levels are set independently of each other.

An effort to apply the arboreal approach to Mamaindé is described later in this paper. However, because of the problems encountered using metrical trees for this data, I will be using only the metrical grid formalism discussed below in my analysis.

5.2. Grid theory. Metrical grids are a different sort of formalism than metrical trees. They depict stress as three (or more) rows of horizontal grid marks placed above the segments in the word. The first row is known as the mora row, where an x is placed above each mora in the string. The second row corresponds to the foot level, where an x is placed over every syllable that is stressed. The final row is at the word level, where a mark is placed only above the syllable that receives the primary stress of the word. The final result is a grid which visually displays the relative degree of prominence assigned to each syllable.

Grid theory also has a very limited set of rules. Like the arboreal approach, these rules consist of only a few parameters which must be set in order to predict stress. They are somewhat different in application to the arboreal rules, but their purposes are quite similar. The four parameters of grid theory, which I use extensively in this paper, are listed in (66).

(66) Parameters of metrical grid theory

    Perfect grid   yes/no
                                      trough first/peak first
                                        right-to-left/left-to-right
    Quantity sensitive   yes/no
    End rule   yes/no
                                        initial/final
                                        foot/word
    Extrametricality   yes/no

The PERFECT GRID PARAMETER simply states whether or not the language has an alternating stress pattern. If the answer is yes, a choice must be made between trough first or peak first, essentially specifying whether the first syllable considered will be stressed (peak first) or unstressed (trough first). The appropriate grid marks are then filled in on the foot row above alternating syllables. Of course, the directionality of application must also be indicated.

The notion of quantity sensitivity has already been discussed. In grid theory, those languages which always stress heavy syllables can be depicted in a graphic way by placing an *x* on the initial row above each mora, typically one above the nucleus and one above the coda position. Then a grid mark is placed on the foot row **only** above the nucleus of each **heavy** syllable.[25]

An example in (67) of a quantity-sensitive language is Damascene Arabic (taken from Goldsmith 1990:202).

(67) Damascene Arabic

    word
    foot   x   x
    mora   x   xx   xx
                  da   *ras* *tuu*

It is possible to distinguish visually between heavy and light syllables by simply looking at the mora row of *x*'s, even though the extra grid mark above the coda is actually not necessary in quantity-sensitive languages unless they also have perfect grid applying. In that case, the

---

[25]In such representations, each row of stress marks is labeled by the structure at which that row is evident. For example, *m* mora row, *f* foot row, and *w* word row. The word level stress has been omitted in example (67).

An Overview of Metrical Phonology 51

x's above the coda are essential because the rule of perfect grid must count each mora in its alternating pattern across the word.

Goldsmith (1990:193) describes the end rule as nothing more than a mechanism "which places a grid mark on the extreme left or extreme right of whatever domain it is specified for." The end of the string which receives the stress must be specified as either [initial] or [final]. The level at which this rule applies must also be stated, whether at the foot or word levels. Thus a complete end rule (abbreviated ER) might look like that in (68):

(68) ER [final, foot]

This rule would apply a grid mark above the last syllable of the string at the foot level. If, however, this rule were changed to ER [final, word], the x would not necessarily be added to the last syllable of the word, but instead to the last syllable which has already received a foot level stress. In other words, the word level is oblivious to any material which is not stressed at the foot level (and in the same way, foot level rules have access only to those segments carrying a mora-level mark), and therefore can only continue to build the stress grid upon marks which already exist on the row just beneath it. Applying the following parameters to the string, *Alabama* would look like the grids in (69)–(70).

(69) At the foot-level

   Perfect grid [peak-first, left-right]

   w
   f   x   x
   m   x   x   x   x
       a   la   ba   ma

(70) At the word-level

   End rule [final, word]

   w   x
   f   x   x
   m   x   x   x   x
       a   la ba   ma

Extrametricality is the last parameter which must be set. As in the arboreal approach, the rules which build grid structure are oblivious to the presence of such extrametrical syllables. In the grid method, the presence of extrametrical material is indicated by placing parentheses around the mora level grid marks of the syllables in question. Any further grid marks are not allowed to be placed above such syllables. Note example (71).

(71) Cairene Arabic (from Goldsmith 1990:200)

```
w      x
f   x  x
m   x  xx  (x)
   ka  tab  ti      final syllable is extrametrical
```

6
A Metrical Analysis of Mamaindé Stress

As in any linguistic problem, the more universal or unmarked solution is always preferred over the unique or more marked case. Therefore, I will now attempt the simplest solution to the Mamaindé problem, which is to look at the entire word as a whole and apply the principles of metrical phonology after the morphology has been completed. This seems to be the locus of most stress rules cross-linguistically.

Consider the word in (72). (I am assuming that the process of syllabification has already applied in this example.)

(72) ['sux."ton.ta.'let.nan.wa]   'it was not known to me'

Using metrical theory, I would first establish Mamaindé as a QUANTITY-SENSITIVE language, so that all heavy syllables attract stress. This is shown visually in (73) by placing an x over each mora, which makes a clear distinction between light and heavy syllables (those with two x's are heavy, those with only one x are light).

(73) mora row   xx xx x xx xx x
          sux.ton.ta.let.nan.wa

Secondly, the foot-level stress rule is shown in (74). It would apply foot stress only on heavy syllables; note (75).

(74) [QS, yes]

(75) foot row   x   x   x   x
      mora row   xx xx x xx xx   x
                   sux.ton.ta.let.nan.wa

    This rule, however, has two drawbacks. By looking at the original word, ['sux."ton.ta.'let.nan.wa], it is obvious that there is a problem with the penultimate syllable in that it should not receive any stress. The only way within the theory to handle this is to posit *nan* as an extrametrical syllable, one which is not considered for stress placement, even though it is heavy.[26] As was noted in chapter 1, however, most linguists tend to agree that extrametricality must be limited to only the most peripheral element of a string, either the right-most or the left-most (see Goldsmith 1990:212–214 and Hayes 1981:82 for discussion). We noted earlier that this peripherality condition, which was proposed by Harris (1982), seems to hold over a major portion of the languages studied. However, *nan,* in the word above, is not located at a word boundary. Therefore, in order to maintain the peripherality condition, the last two syllables must be considered as extrametrical in this verb as in (76).

(76)   '*sux"tonta'let(nanwa)*   'it was not known to me'

But in other verbs, such as the one in (77), there are no extrametrical syllables.

(77)   "*xai'texna'tax*   'in order to go'

How can it be determined when the last two syllables of a verb are extrametrical and when they are not? Clearly something is amiss in the analysis. The only way a generalization could be captured here is to appeal to morphology and consider all members of the person/tense/aspect system as extrametrical (*nan* and *wa* are members of this set whereas *texnatax* is not). Although this would work, the question arises whether this is a valid use of the notion EXTRAMETRICAL. Hayes (1981:82) argues that, in order to constrain the theory, the use of extrametricality should be limited to marking only structural

---

[26]There are some languages in which sonorant codas are not assigned a mora and therefore such syllables are never considered heavy. This is not what is going on here, however, as many syllables with sonorant codas are considered heavy in Mamaindé, such as *ton* in the above example.

constituents, such as segments or syllables, not morphemes. Goldsmith (1990:213) also agrees that extrametricality, at least in English, should be oblivious to morphological categories, although he does allow extrametricality to refer to word classes (recall that nouns in English have a final extrametrical syllable, as in the word *'elas"tici(ty)* discussed in chapter 5). But referring to morpheme classes (as opposed to word classes) in a particular rule actually seems no different than positing a separate lexical stratum where that rule applies. But if we are going to hold to the position that stress follows morphology, then we must be willing to accept the existence of several extrametrical syllables at the right-end of many Mamaindé words. The number of these syllables would then vary, depending on the syntactic class of each morpheme involved. I believe this is stretching the definition of extrametricality to a point where it can do almost anything, and thus can explain virtually nothing. A final blow to the application of extrametricality in Mamaindé is the existence of some forms which actually do stress these person/tense/aspect morphemes which otherwise appear to be extrametrical, such as *na-'nax-wa* 'I am' and *na-'latha-wa* 'He/she/it is'.

The other drawback of the QS foot rule is that it requires vowel length to be added to the underlying forms of some lexical items in order for the correct syllables to be considered as heavy for stress placement. For example, for the word in (78), the underlying form of the root morpheme *halo* 'land' would have to be included in the lexicon with the final vowel already lengthened. Otherwise there would not be any heavy syllables in the string and the quantity sensitive (QS) rule would not apply to this word at all.

(78)　Application of QS rule

　　　　with underlying　　　　　without underlying
　　　　vowel length　　　　　　 vowel length

　　　　　x
　　　x xx　x　　　　　　　　　x x　x
　　　/ha.lo:.-txu/　　　　　　 /ha.lo.-txu/ *

I believe this to be an undesirable result of this approach, since specifying vowel length in the underlying root proves to be totally unnecessary when using the correct analysis, as will be seen in chapter 8.

Even if the problems of extrametricality and vowel length at the foot level could be resolved, it would be necessary to write a rule for word-level stress. Doing this without reference to morphology, however, proves impossible. First of all, there is no way to write a rule that can assign primary stress to its proper place, since it can occur to the right of, to the left of, or even between secondary stresses, as seen in the forms in (79).

(79)   "x<u>a</u>isa'toxni   'if going'
       'kax"y<u>ā</u>isaxwa   'I write'
       'sux"tonta'letnanwa 'I didn't know'

Further, primary stress is often found juxtaposed to another primary stress within the same word, e.g., 'ika"la:"kuh'texna'tax 'in order to work with'. The usual parameters with which word-level stress is assigned, such as right-headed or left-headedness, end rule, and perfect grid, would clearly not apply to this system. In fact, it is not clear that there is any word-level rule that would work given the basic assumption of this approach, namely, that stress does not appeal to morphology. Therefore, a more powerful approach to Mamaindé stress is needed, combining the rules of metrical phonology with the morphological processes of lexical phonology. Chapter 7 gives a brief summary of the theory of lexical phonology and chapter 8 discusses the application of this theory to Mamaindé stress.

7
An Overview of Lexical Phonology

The theory of lexical phonology has become well-known through the work of Mohanan (1986) and others.[27] At the heart of this approach is the intentional marriage of phonology with morphology, bringing back into focus the larger domain of phonology, namely, the syntactic categories in which it functions. This is done by first distinguishing between phonological rule applications which require access to morphological information and those that do not. The former are said to belong to the LEXICAL COMPONENT, and the latter to the POST-LEXICAL COMPONENT. Within the lexical component, phonological operations and morphological operations alternate, each producing an input to the other. This alternating process is organized by means of STRATA, which can be defined as subsequent stages in the derivation of a word which have their own unique set of phonological rules and morpheme affixation processes. Thus each phonological rule within the lexical component must be identified as belonging to a particular stratum, and likewise each affixation process must be identified as to which stratum it belongs. When a root morpheme enters the first stratum, it undergoes those affixation processes found within that stratum which are applicable, and is then subjected to each phonological rule of that stratum. It then enters the next stratum, where more affixes and rules are applied, and so on

---

[27]This chapter is based on Mohanan's *Theory of Lexical Phonology* 1986.

through every stratum until it emerges from the lexical component as a completed word with all the affixation and appropriate phonology done.

The unique claim of lexical phonology, then, is that many phonological processes actually take place during the morphology, i.e., while the word is being built, as opposed to being restricted to a post-morphological application as is the case in classical generative phonological theory. The obvious advantage to this view of phonology is that it cuts down considerably on the amount of context which is present at the time the lexical rules apply. This in turn enables the rules themselves to be simplified. But the greatest advantage of lexical phonology is that it provides a formalized structure within which rules may be written that apply to specific morpheme classes without overburdening the lexicon. Without a lexical view of phonology, morpheme-specific rules are actually no more than another way of saying that a specific set of morphemes must have its underlying forms altered in a certain way within the lexicon. Kingston's stress rules in chapter 4, for example, essentially are adding different stress levels to the underlying forms of each morpheme class. Although this method does capture the basic idea of Mamaindé stress, that it is governed by morphology, it seems to complicate the underlying representations in a way that is not necessary with a lexical approach.

Of course, lexical phonology also allows for rules which make no reference to morphology. These are said to belong to the post-lexical component. This is the locus of phonological processes that apply to fully completed words, such as simple phonetic alternations and phrase level rules. Thus, after a word leaves the lexical component, it enters the post-lexical component for fine tuning. The output of the post-lexical component is then the output of the whole phonology. This process is diagrammed in (80).

An Overview of Lexical Phonology

(80) Model of lexical phonology

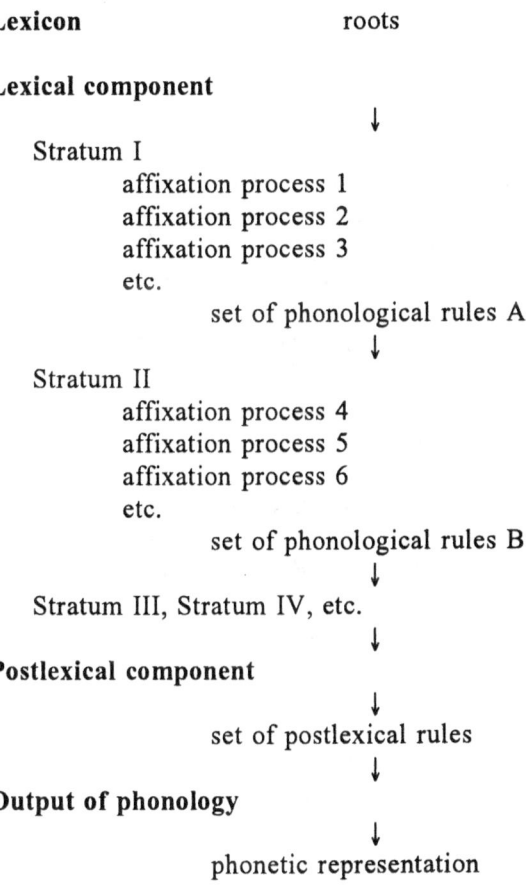

A few further notions must be made clear. The order in which phonological rules and affixation processes apply within a given stratum serve to classify that stratum as being CYCLICAL or NONCYCLICAL. A cyclical stratum is one in which all of its rules apply each time a new morpheme is added within that stratum. Noncyclical strata, on the other hand, are those whose phonological rules apply only after all the morphology of that stratum has been done, as was represented in the model of lexical phonology in (80). The illustration in (81) shows the model of lexical phonology modified to include cyclical strata.

(81) Model of lexical phonology with cyclical strata

Lexicon   roots

Lexical component
↓

   Stratum I
       affixation process 1
           set of phonological rules A
       affixation process 2
           set of phonological rules A
       affixation process 3
           set of phonological rules A
       etc.
            ↓

   Stratum II
       affixation process 4
           set of phonological rules B
       affixation process 5
           set of phonological rules B
       affixation process 6
           set of phonological rules B
       etc.
            ↓

Postlexical component
↓
       set of postlexical rules
↓
Output of phonology
↓

       phonetic representation

The STRICT CYCLE CONDITION, or STRICT CYCLICITY, has been formalized by Kiparsky (1982) to restrict the theory and explain why some lexical rules fail to apply. This condition states that "a lexical rule will not change a feature value in a non-derived context" (Goldsmith 1990:245). Basically, this allows a lexical rule to apply only if morphological material has been added during that stratum, creating a derived environment. The operative principle here is that lexical rules must apply to a given morpheme at the time that morpheme enters the phonology, or in other words, after the first cycle in which it is present in the lexical component. This first-chance-only type of rule application means that if a certain morpheme from stratum I enters stratum II without acquiring any affixes from stratum II, then the stratum II lexical rules are not allowed to apply to that morpheme since it was not derived in stratum II. To put it simply, if the affixation processes of a particular stratum do not apply to a given form, neither can the phonological rules of that stratum apply.

Another restriction which seems to hold across languages is that no rule can apply only in non-adjacent strata. For example, a given phonological process which applies in stratum I may not apply in stratum III without also being present for potential application in stratum II. However, the same rule is allowed to apply both in the lexical component and in the postlexical component.

The only new formalism introduced by this theory is a special use of brackets. These brackets are used to mark the boundaries of the domains in which rules are allowed to apply. Initially, all morphemes in the lexicon are placed in brackets which mark the boundaries of that morpheme (just as + and − did in standard phonology). When an affix is added to a root by a morphological rule, they are both placed within one pair of brackets while keeping their individual brackets. The outside brackets mark the domain of application for any subsequent rules, and the internal brackets show the boundaries of each morpheme. After each cycle, the internal brackets are deleted, signifying that the output of each cycle no longer has any visible morpheme boundaries. The result is that the string is considered by the next cycle as a single indivisible form, lacking any internal morphological structure. This process is known as BRACKET ERASURE (or BE for short) and must apply at the end of each cycle. For example, the word *unbelievable* would be bracketed as in (82).

(82) Bracket erasure convention

	[un]	[believe]	[able]
Cycle 1			
affixation		[[believe][able]]	
bracket erasure		[believable]	
Cycle 2			
affixation		[[un][believable]]	
bracket erasure		[unbelievable]	

Although I use bracket erasure throughout this paper for the sake of clarity, it is actually unnecessary to use this bracket convention when strict cyclicity is assumed. As was mentioned earlier, strict cyclicity allows lexical rules to apply only to forms derived in their stratum.

There are other important claims made by the theory of lexical phonology, such as the UNDERSPECIFICATION OF FEATURES, which I do not address here since they are irrelevant to our discussion.

8
A Lexical Analysis of Mamaindé Stress

I discussed in chapter 6 why the stress system of Mamaindé cannot be explained by using the usual method, i.e., metrical phonology, alone. It is necessary to add a more complicated apparatus to the analysis, namely, lexical phonology. Although lexical phonology is perhaps too powerful at times (Goldsmith 1990:6), it appears to be the only theoretical framework by which Mamaindé stress can be predicted. This fact alone makes lexical phonology a valid system.

The purpose of this section is to show that stress in Mamaindé is not a postmorphological process. It is in fact the result of a set of rules that apply during the morphology of each word, such that when all of the affixes have been attached, stress assignment has also been completed.

8.1. The lexical strata. To account for the diverse stress patterns found in this language, Mamaindé phonology must be considered to consist of two components: a lexical component (that part of phonology which applies during the morphological construction of words) and a postlexical component (phonological processes which occur after words have been constructed). For Mamaindé, the lexical component itself must then be subdivided into four separate, cyclical strata, where each stratum is differentiated by a distinct set of affixes and phonological stress rules.

The strata of Mamaindé phonology with the stress rules are listed in (83). These rules are explained in §§8.2–8.3. They are listed here in

(83) Mamaindé stress rules in the lexical model

    LEXICAL COMPONENT
    Stratum I
        Affixation processes
            Cycles: 1. root only
                         2. prefixes (including reduplicated prefixes)
                         3. infixes
                         4. compounds
        Phonological stress rules
            Quantity sensitivity (QS)
            End rule [final, foot] (ERFF)
            End rule [final, word] (ERFW)
    Stratum II
        Affixation processes
            Cycles: 1. auxiliary suffixes
                         2. prepositions
                         3. object markers
        Phonological stress rules
            Quantity sensitivity (QS)
            End rule [final, word] (ERFW)
    Stratum III
        Affixation processes
            Cycles: 1. modifiers
                         2. noun classifiers
                         3. conjunctions
                         4. connectives
        Phonological stress rules
            Quantity sensitivity (QS)
    Stratum IV
        Affixation processes
            Cycles: 1. subject markers
                         2. tense markers
                         3. mood markers
                         4. articles
        Phonological stress rules
            none in this stratum

    POSTLEXICAL COMPONENT
        Phonological stress rules
            End rule [initial, foot] (ERIF)
            Phrase level stress rules

order to show the manner in which the Mamaindé morphology and phonology are interwoven.

It is important to keep in mind that these are all cyclical strata, and thus all the phonological rules in a given stratum apply after each cycle of affixation in that stratum. In reality, then, the ordering of the above processes looks more like the list in (84) below.

(84) LEXICAL COMPONENT
    Stratum I
    Cycle 1
        Affixation process: root only
        Phonological stress rules—Set A
            Quantity sensitivity (QS)
            End rule [final, foot] (ERFF)
            End rule [final, word] (ERFW)
    Cycle 2
        Affixation process: prefixes (including reduplicated prefixes)
        Phonological stress rules—Set A
            Quantity sensitivity (QS)
            End rule [final, foot] (ERFF)
            End rule [final, word] (ERFW)
    Cycle 3
        Affixation process: infixes
        Phonological stress rules—Set A
            Quantity sensitivity (QS)
            End rule [final, foot] (ERFF)
            End rule [final, word] (ERFW)
    Cycle 4
        Affixation process: compounds
        Phonological stress rules—Set A
            Quantity sensitivity (QS)
            End rule [final, foot] (ERFF)
            End rule [final, word] (ERFW)
    Stratum II
    Cycle 1
        Affixation process: auxiliary suffixes
        Phonological stress rules—Set B
            Quantity sensitivity (QS)
            End rule [final, word] (ERFW)

Cycle 2
      Affixation process: prepositions
      Phonological stress rules—Set B
         Quantity sensitivity (QS)
         End rule [final, word] (ERFW)
   Cycle 3
      Affixation process: object markers
      Phonological stress rules—Set B
         Quantity sensitivity (QS)
         End rule [final, word] (ERFW)
   etc.

Although not mentioned in the discussion above, it is assumed that the natural processes of syllabification, which include the maximization of onsets, and the vowel lengthening 1 rule of chapter 2, are applied in a persistent manner as the first phonological rules after every affixation process in every stratum, as well as in the postlexical component.

Before getting into the detail of the rules, it is necessary to be sure that the basis for this stratal division is clear. The motivation for positing these different strata comes from the fact that these four groups of morphemes receive different degrees of stress. Stratum I and II morphemes can receive primary stress or secondary stress; stratum III morphemes can receive only secondary stress; and stratum IV morphemes receive no stress at all (except under a special condition to be mentioned later). Furthermore, each stratum can be defined by appealing to natural morpheme classes. In effect, I have simply reiterated Kingston's basic assumption that the different levels of stress in this language are conditioned by morphology.

Considering the phonological processes applying in the list above, stratum I can be distinguished from II, III, and IV because the ERFF rule is operative only within stratum I. Stratum II can be established as distinct from III and IV by the presence of the ERFW rule. The QS rule is present in stratum III but not in IV. And of course, in stratum IV, none of the stress rules apply.

Thus on both morphological and phonological grounds, the four strata can be established. A list of some of the morphemes used in this paper, organized according to their stratum and cycle is given in (85) (the first number indicates the stratum while the second indicates the cycle).

A Lexical Analysis of Mamaindé Stress

(85) List of morphemes by strata and cycle

1—1 stems

x<u>a</u>i	'to go'	sun	'father-in-law'
w<u>a</u>	'to come'	halo	'land'
kala	'to work, to raise'	tanu	'to give'
on	'to do'	tu	'to get'
set/sen	'to speak'	y<u>a</u>u	'to stay, live'
wet	'child'	na	'to be, to say' or pro-verb (no meaning)
wanũn	'good'		

1—2 prefixes

ta	'my'
na	'his'
wa	'your'
nusa	'our'
i	(causative)
ma	(reduplicating prefix)

1—3 infixes

lo	(reduplicating infix)

1—4 compounds

The list of stems found in cycle 1—1

2—1 auxiliary suffixes

ten	'will'
yex	'surely'
nun	'not'
hen	'time'

2—2 prepositions

ka	'for'
kuh	'with'

2—3 object markers

ta	(1p obj.)
xna	(2p obj.)
∅	(3p obj.)
lex	(1ppl obj.)

3—1 modifiers

let	'did'
iyah	'that one'

3—2 noun class

si	'group'
i	'animate'
sokx	'person'

3—3 conjunctions

texnatax	'in order to'
takxu	'and'
khatox	'then'

4—1 subject markers

ax/nax	'1p subj.'
nnax/nux/nun	'2p subj.'
latha	'3p subj.'

4—2 tense

nan	(recent past)
∅	(present)
nun	(future)

4—3 mood/articles

txu	'a'
anxi	'the'
wa	(declarative)

Interesting examples which support the existence of these lexical strata are forms like those in (86).

(86) /"wa.nun.ta.wa/   'you obviously will come'
    /wa."nũn.ax.wa/   'I am good'

There is no way these forms could receive these two different stress patterns from a postlexical perspective since they have the same number of syllables, and also have identical environments in the first two syllables where a difference in stress occurs.[28] Only by referring to lexical strata can we understand the major difference in these words. First of all, /"wa-nun-ta-wa/ contains the monosyllabic root /wa/, whereas /wa"nũn-ax-wa/ has the bisyllabic root /wanũn/. These roots both belong to the initial stratum, where stress rules (which are described in the next section) place stress on the last heavy syllable in the root, or on the last syllable if none are heavy. Therefore stress occurs on the monosyllabic root /"wa/ and on the second syllable of the root /wa."nũn/. The other morphemes in both words belong to stratum IV, where none of the stress rules apply. This explains why /nun/ in the first word and /ax/ in the second word do not attract stress even though they are heavy syllables. The end result is a correct prediction of stress on these two forms by applying the stress rules to the stratum I morphemes and not to stratum IV morphemes, just as the description of Mamaindé lexical strata would suggest.

Other forms that support a stratal approach to Mamaindé stress are those which contain first and second person subject markers. These markers are /ax/ and /nax/ respectively when the previous syllable has been stressed, as in /"wa-ax-wa/ 'I am going'. However, if the previous syllable lacks stress, these subject markers are then realized as /nax/ and /nux/ respectively, as in /'i-ka"la-ka-nax-wa/ 'I am working'. The interesting thing about these variations in person markers is that the morphology of the language must somehow "know" whether or not the previous syllable has been stressed before it can add the subject marker suffix. This could only be the case if the stress rules have already applied before the subject marker is affixed to the string. Thus the stress rules must be part of the lexical component of this language, and they must belong to a stratum prior to the affixation of subject markers. That is exactly what is predicted, as can be seen in the outline of the lexical strata above. Such forms, then, constitute strong evidence for a lexical analysis of Mamaindé stress.

---

[28]The variations in nasal and laryngeal prosody here have no effect on stress placement. Rather, stress is applied first and then other autosegmental features such as nasality tend to choose stressed vowels as their prosody-bearing units.

A Lexical Analysis of Mamaindé Stress

8.2–8.3 The Lexical Rules

The next two sections (§§8.2–8.3) present the specific rules which determine stress placement in Mamaindé. The parameters of metrical grid theory are used throughout.

8.2. Rules of the lexical component. First of all this is a quantity-sensitive language. This characteristic is depicted on the metrical grid by assigning an x above every mora (one for each nucleus and coda position). The four morphemes *wankha* 'to return', *halo* 'land', *suxton* 'not knowing', and *tu* 'to get' are used as examples. Since these forms are all roots, they all belong to the first cycle of the first stratum.

The initial assignment of the mora row does not constitute a stress rule as such; it simply follows from the fact that this language must have a way to distinguish between light and heavy syllables. Whether the mora row is specified in the lexicon or not is a moot point. In all the derivations in this paper, the mora row will be filled in at the time a morpheme enters the lexical component. Thus we have the mora row in (87).

(87) word row
    foot row
    mora row   xx x   x x   xx xx   x
                     wan.kha   ha.lo   sux.ton   tu

Then we apply the first foot-level stress rule, rule 1.

(88) **Rule 1. Quantity sensitive rule [yes]** (QS)

The effect of the QS rule is to apply a foot-level stress above the nucleus of every heavy syllable, illustrated in (89).

(89) Application of QS rule

    w
    f   x   x x
    m   xx x   x x   xx xx   x
         wan.kha   ha.lo   sux.ton   tu

The second and fourth roots still have not received stress. Therefore rule 1 must be paired with rule 2.

(90) **Rule 2. End rule [final, foot]** (ERFF)

Rule 2 applies a foot level stress mark on the right-most syllable. However, these first two rules are ordered in their application by the ELSEWHERE CONDITION (Kiparsky 1973), which gives priority in assigning foot-level stress to the more specific rule. Since the QS rule is concerned only with the internal make-up of individual syllables, while the ERFF rule must look at the whole string, the domain of the QS rule is a subset of the domain of the ERFF rule. The QS rule, then, is the more specific rule and must be given priority. Goldsmith (1990:189–90) mentions this same relationship between these two rules and adds the following statement.

> Thus, the idea that the stress assigned by the second, quantity-insensitive, rule is a 'default' rule, picking up the pieces left over by the quantity-sensitive rule, is recognized by the theory.

The ERFF rule therefore only applies when QS fails to apply, as shown in (91).

(91) Application of ERFF rule

```
w
f   x              x   x  x      x
m   xx    x        x x  xx xx    x
    wan.kha    ha.lo  sux.ton    tu
```

Notice that in the first and third roots ERFF does not apply because QS has already assigned foot level stress. In the second and fourth examples, where QS failed to apply, ERFF is invoked and stresses the final syllable. (Monosyllabic roots such as *tu* receive stress by this ERFF rule since the one and only syllable is also considered the final syllable.)

The effect of these two foot-level rules, then, is that all heavy syllables receive foot-level stress, or if none are heavy, then the last syllable receives the foot-level stress.

Although the pairing of these two rules is not a typical way to assign foot-level stress, Goldsmith (1990:188–89) observes these same two rules functioning together in Aguacatec Mayan, where on the foot-level all heavy syllables are stressed, or else the last syllable if none are heavy. The only difference between the stress system of this language and Mamaindé is that in Aguacatec these rules apply to the whole word, whereas in Mamaindé they are limited to the morphological structures of certain strata.

Although some surface forms actually have phonetically lengthened vowels, such as [haloː] 'land' and [tuː] 'to get', the Mamaindé stress system is able to apply foot-level stress to these two roots correctly without resorting to the postulative of lengthened vowels in the lexicon. This is one advantage to this lexical analysis. By using the notion of strata it is possible to determine which light syllables need to be stressed by the ERFF rule. Length on these particular vowels can then easily be added later by rule. Without allowing the phonology rules to apply during the morphology of the word, however, it would be necessary to write stress rules which could only view the Mamaindé word as a whole, and thus morpheme boundaries would be invisible. This would then require an addition of length to the last vowel of such underlying forms as /halo/ and /tu/, making them /haloː/ and /tuː/ respectively in the lexicon. That would be the only way for the stress rules to distinguish them from any other vowel. The use of strata and the ERFF rule, however, make this unnecessary. This is one reason why using the lexical theory of phonology makes for a better analysis in this language.

The next step is to assign word level stress by applying rule 3.

(92) **Rule 3. End rule [final, word]** (ERFW)

The effect of this end rule is to apply a word level stress on the right-most syllable available. Following standard interpretation, available refers to that set of syllables which have already received a grid mark on the foot level and are therefore considered as legitimate building blocks for higher levels of stress. Word level stress is consequently blind to any other syllables which have not already been stressed on the foot level.

This means that, although end rule is [final, word], some morphemes will actually receive word level stress on the final syllable while others may not, e.g., (93).

(93) w   x
   f x x   x x
     m xx xx   xx xx
         sux.ton   →   *sux.ton*

```
w                      x
f    x                 x
m    x  x              x  x
     ha.lo       →     ha.lo


w                      x
f    x                 x
m    xx  x       →     xx  x
     wan.kha           wan.kha
```

The last morpheme in example (93) receives word-level stress on the first syllable instead of the last because /wan/ is the rightmost (and only) syllable that has a foot level grid mark. The last syllable /kha/ is not available for word-level stress because it lacks foot-level stress.

Note that rules 1, 2, and 3, taken together, will basically apply word-level stress to the right-most heavy syllable, or else to the last syllable if none are heavy. Aguacatec Mayan uses this same strategy for applying word-level stress.

Mamaindé does not have a perfect grid rule and therefore the setting of this parameter would be as in (94).

(94) Perfect grid [no]

This means that there is no regular alternating pattern of stress active in this language. However, a small tendency in this direction is discussed later.

Notice that the extrametricality rule that was necessary in the analysis considered in chapter 6 is no longer required; the strata themselves produce the desired result. Although it might appear that the last stratum, where none of the stress rules apply, is simply a way to hide extrametricality, I believe the use of strata is actually more predictive than that interpretation suggests. The reason the extrametricality rule was difficult to formulate in the previous approach was that it ignored the fact that the basis for lack of stress in various penultimate and final syllables is not structural, but morphological. The strata are not being used to hide anything, but to allow for a systematic way of referring to various morpheme classes. The lack of an extrametricality rule is therefore significant here in that it makes the current analysis simpler by one less rule (and an awkward one at that).

The application of these rules is straightforward, except that the strata in which they apply must be specified. This crucial notion of strata

A Lexical Analysis of Mamaindé Stress

which divide the morpheme classes is the distinctive feature of this analysis over a more standard metrical approach, and it is exactly this addition to the theory that allows the Mamaindé stress rules to work precisely. In other words, these metrical rules are useless in Mamaindé unless the domain in which they are operative is specified.

I do not attempt to hide the fact that these strata are essentially divisions of morphemes. As unappealing as it may sound, there is no way to avoid a direct use of morphology in the application of Mamaindé stress, as Kingston ("Mamaindé Syllables") predicted.

8.3. Rules of the postlexical component. Another set of rules applies to the word after it has left the morphology. These rules make phonetic modifications (including stress) to the string both at the whole word and phrase levels. Together, they make up the postlexical component of the phonology.

(95) **Rule 4. End rule [initial, foot]** (ERIF)

Rule 4 applies a foot-level grid mark above the first syllable of a string which has entered the postlexical component. However, there is a further requirement: there must be two unstressed syllables at the beginning of the string for this rule to apply.

This is obviously a very restricted rule, and thus undesirable from a metrical theory point of view. The environment for this rule is stated overtly here only for the purpose of clarity, however, and after I have dicussed WELL-FORMEDNESS STATEMENTS in chapter 11, it will be seen that such an awkward statement is not necessary at all, for the environment of this rule follows from universal tendencies which do not need to be made language-specific.

A derivation of the form /ˈwahaⁿlotxu/ 'your land', including application of rule 4, is given in (96). The abbreviation N/A marks any stratum or rule which does not apply. (The process of bracket erasure is also included in this and all subsequent derivations. However, this is a mere formalism and not a rule as such, and in fact included here only as an aid to clarity.)

(96) /wa/ + /halo/ + /txu/   'your' + 'land' + 'indefinite article'

    LEXICAL COMPONENT
    Stratum I
    Cycle 1
      affixation

```
                    x x
        root [halo]
     rules
         QS      N/A
                     x
                    x x
        ERFF [halo]
                     x
                     x
                    x x
        ERFW [halo]
```

    Cycle 2
      affixation

```
                          x
                          x
                    x    x x
        prefix [[wa][halo]]
     rules
         QS      N/A
         ERFF    N/A
         ERFW    N/A
                       x
                       x
                     x x x
        BE      [wahalo]
```

Stratum II
N/A
Stratum III
N/A

A Lexical Analysis of Mamaindé Stress

Stratum IV
Cycle 3
affixation

```
                    x
                    x
              x x x   x
   article [[wahalo][txu]]
```
rules
   no rules in this stratum
```
              x
              x
              x x x x
   BE [wahalotxu]
```

POSTLEXICAL COMPONENT
rules
```
              x
            x   x
            x x x x
   ERIF [wahalotxu]
```

The form arrived at under the postlexical component is the correct form. Note that the ERIF rule applied since neither of the first two syllables had received any stress during the lexical component of the phonology. Apparently Mamaindé does not permit a span of two unstressed syllables at the beginning of the word.[29] Elsewhere in the string,

---

[29]The only exception to this rule that has been found to date is the form [wa.le."khan.txu] 'chief'. This word lacks stress on the first two syllables, but ERIF has not applied. Note, however, that this is a rare form in the language, as it contains a three-syllable root, *walekhan*. Virtually all other roots are one or two syllables in length. An interesting thing happens, though, when we add a prefix, such as *ta-* 'my', to this three-syllable root. It becomes /'ta.wa.le."khan.txu/ 'my chief'. The ERIF rule has now applied to this form, placing a foot-level stress on the first syllable. This suggests that the ERIF rule is triggered only by the addition of a prefix. (This seems to hold true in other examples as well, such as /'wa.ha."lo.txu/ 'your land', which also contains a prefix.) If this proves to be so, prefixes must be placed in a separate stratum of their own, and have the ERIF rule apply only within that stratum. Thus only those forms which actually add a prefix would be possible candidates for the ERIF rule. The condition requiring two unstressed syllables in the beginning of the string must still be enforced, however, as prefixed forms such as /ta."hukx.txu/ 'my bow' never receive stress on the first syllable. It appears possible, then, that ERIF applies only when a prefix creates a span of two unstressed syllables word

however, such a pattern is permissible and actually common. Consider the words in (97), for example.

(97) [ta."nu:.ta.la.tha.wa]   'he gave to me'
     ["on.ka.kha.'tox]   'work for, then'

The ERIF rule is therefore necessary to apply an initial foot-level stress to those forms which have left the lexical component without any stress on the first two syllables.

This rule is also used to apply stress to certain forms which have escaped the stress rules altogether. These totally unstressed words are then stressed on the first syllable by the ERIF rule of the postlexical component. (A detailed discussion of these unstressed strings is found later in this chapter in conjunction with the insert [a] rule.)

It is interesting to note that rule 4, the last stress rule, is end rule [initial] rather than [final], as all other end rules have been. At first glance this may appear to be an undesirable addition to the stress system, seemingly changing the whole nature of the Mamaindé stress pattern, which has always stressed the final syllable of a given domain, to suddenly begin stressing the initial syllable in what seems to be an arbitrary way. But it is exactly the issue of "domain" which is relevant here. Keep in mind that this rule applies only in the postlexical component after all the morphology has been completed. Therefore, its domain is the whole word. On the other hand, the domains of the lexical rules are much smaller, and although they stress the final syllable in their domains, in terms of the whole word, they tend to be closer to, if not exactly on, the left edge of the string. This is because the word-level stress rules are operative only in the first two strata and not the last two. The result of these lexical strata is that Mamaindé words, at least most of them, apparently prefer to have the higher stressed syllables closer to the beginning of the word and the lower stressed syllables toward the end of the word, often finishing the string with several totally unstressed syllables. Of course, there are many exceptions to this tendency, particularly when the word does not have any stratum III and stratum IV suffixes. Nevertheless, it is a tendency. Therefore, this ERIF rule in the postlexical component is actually attempting to follow a pattern already

---

initially. Unfortunately, to treat prefixes separately in this way would add a fifth stratum to the lexical component, thereby further complicating the phonology, something which I hesitate to do on the basis of one word which does not fit the present model. At this point I will hold to the four-strata analysis, being fully aware, however, that five strata may be required for this language if further examples of this type are found.

A Lexical Analysis of Mamaindé Stress

established by the strata; it stresses the initial syllable of any string which has escaped the lexical stress rules, thereby placing the stress in the most acceptable location in the string, the place usually occupied by the root. (This ERIF rule is also motivated by tendencies broader than Mamaindé itself; see chapter 11.)

All of the stress rules necessary to predict the placement of stress on the vast majority of Mamaindé words have now been presented. There are, however, other rules which apply within the postlexical component which must be mentioned here. They are not stress rules, but some of them rely on the stress rules to supply the environment for their application. Thus they are crucially ordered after the syllabification and stress rules of the lexical component.

The first one is a second vowel lengthening rule. One vowel lengthening rule which applied before stress and after syllabification has already been discussed in chapter 2. This next rule, however, must apply after all stress rules have been applied, and yet immediately before the last resyllabification process.

Earlier it was pointed out that the ERFF rule of the lexical component allows certain light syllables to be stressed without resorting to lengthened vowels in the lexicon. This is because they can later be lengthened in the postlexical component after they have been stressed. Note the example in (98). This lengthening is accomplished by rule 5 in (99).

(98) Lexical component   Postlexical component

```
    w                    x              x
    f    x               x              x
    m   x x             x x            x x
        halo  →         halo  →        halo:
```

(99) **Rule 5. Vowel lengthening 2 (preservation of coda)** (VL-2)

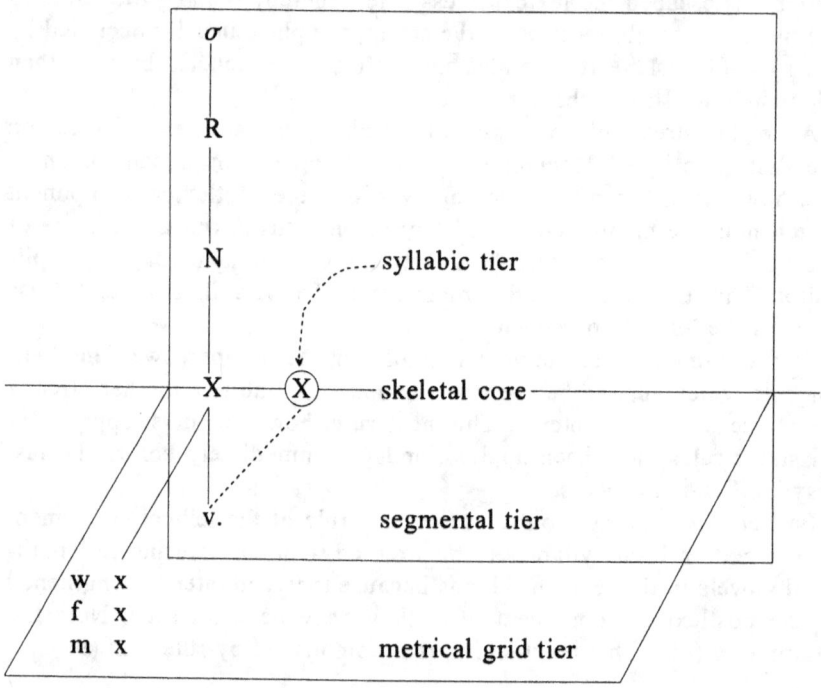

Rule 5 applies to any vowel which meets the above description, i.e., vowels which are followed by a syllable boundary "." and whose skeletal positions are already associated (shown by a solid line) to a word level stress on the metrical grid. Notice that I am depicting the metrical grid as an autosegment located on its own tier and associated to the skeletal tier by association lines. The dotted line shows the effect of the rule, which is to add an extra skeletal position to the right of the vowel and then spread the vowel to it.

The effect of this rule is to lengthen any primary stressed vowel in a light syllable (secondary stressed vowels in light syllables do not get lengthened). The syllable boundary is included as a shorthand way of specifying that this vowel must be the last segment within the syllable. The extra length of the vowel is indicated by an added skeletal position, and the syllable must then build a coda to incorporate this extra skeletal position. This new coda is built by the automatic process of syllabification, which must apply immediately any time new material is added to the segmental or skeletal tiers.

A Lexical Analysis of Mamaindé Stress

The final result of this VL-2 rule and the process of syllabification would look like the diagram in (100).

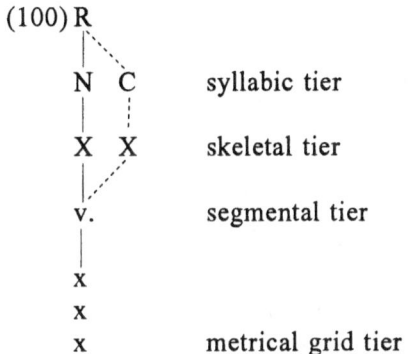

(100)
```
    R
   / \
  N   C      syllabic tier
  |   |
  X   X      skeletal tier
   \ /
    v.       segmental tier
    |
    x
    x
    x        metrical grid tier
```

This coda building process follows from the universal tendency mentioned in Goldsmith (1990:108) that "all segments must be part of a higher-level organization, such as the syllable," and from the laws of syllabic licensing, which require all skeletal positions to be licensed by the syllable in order to be realized on the surface. The alternative to building a coda position would be to allow the extra X to associate to the existing nucleus position, producing a branching nucleus as in (101).

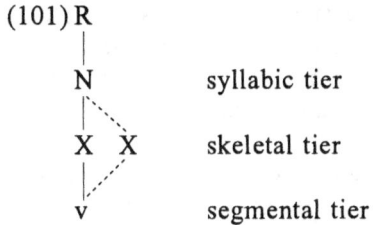

(101)
```
  R
  |
  N          syllabic tier
 / \
X   X        skeletal tier
 \ /
  v          segmental tier
```

This explanation of long vowels in Mamaindé, however, would not allow an important generalization, namely, that all stressed syllables have a branching rhyme, i.e., they must have a coda position. It appears, then, that the principle of quantity sensitivity, where heavy syllables attract stress, is still operative even in the postlexical component, modifying those strings which have escaped the effects of this principle in the lexical component. In essence, Mamaindé phonology is continiously counting the mora of each stressed syllable, and when two mora are not present, it adds one by means of its vowel lengthening rules.

Example (102) shows how the VL-2 rule lengthens those light syllables which were stressed by the ERFF rule. Recall that the ERFF rule stresses the last syllable in root strings which contain only light syllables, where QS has failed to apply.

(102) HA.LO + txu   'land' + 'indefinite article'

    LEXICAL COMPONENT
    Stratum I
    Cycle 1: roots
        QS rule   N/A
        ERFF stress rule   [ha.'lo]
        ERFW stress rule   [ha."lo]

    Stratum IV
    Cycle 4: articles
        no rules here   [ha."lo][txu]

    POSTLEXICAL COMPONENT
        Vowel lengthening rule 2   [ha."lo:txu]

We have seen that although Mamaindé is a quantity-sensitive language, stressing heavy syllables, the stress rules (in particular, ERFF) can also stress some light syllables. The VL-2 rule then comes along and tidies up those light syllables, lengthening the vowel and making all of the primary stressed syllables equally heavy before they leave the phonology. This shows the extent to which quantity sensitivity influences this language.

As mentioned before, this VL-2 rule, coupled with the ERFF rule, also enables us to remove all lengthened vowels from the lexicon, thereby simplifying underlying representations and the list of phonemes necessary to characterize them. Clearly this is an improvement on my earlier analysis.

At this point it will be useful also to consider the coda lengthening rule mentioned in chapter 2. It should be included here since it applies in the postlexical component after all the stress rules, and only affects the structure of the syllable. This rule (rule 6) is necessary to account for the extra length in the codas of words such as those listed in (103). A diagram of rule 6 is given in (104).

A Lexical Analysis of Mamaindé Stress

(103) /hukx/ + /txu/ → [hukx:.txu] 'a bow'
/khatx/ + /txu/ → [khatx:.txu] 'a stick'
/hãn/ + /takxu/ → [hãn:.takxu] 'to be white'

This extra lengthening of consonant codas is not only common in Mamaindé but also in its closest relative, Southern Nambiquára (Kroeker 1976).

(104) **Rule 6. Coda lengthening rule (CL)**

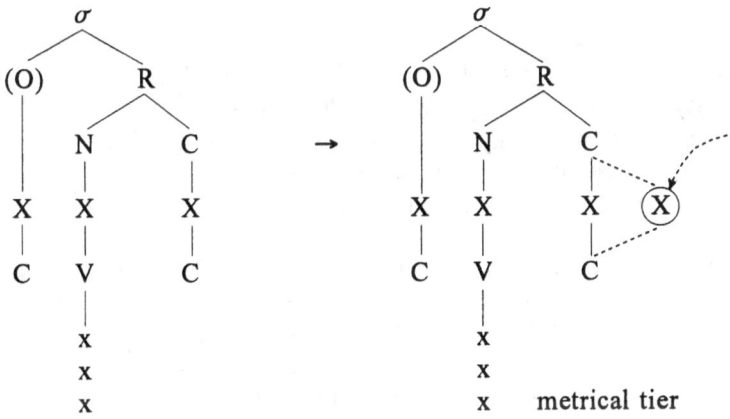

Basically, this (phonetic) rule states that whenever there is a primary stressed syllable with a coda position filled by a consonant, an extra skeletal position is added to the coda, and the single coda segment associates to both of these positions, thus effectively lengthening the consonant. This rule applies only in the postlexical component and consequently does not affect stress or syllable weight. It is crucially ordered after syllabification, and before the pre-stopped nasal rules discussed in Eberhard 1993.

The final postlexical rules which must be discussed are associated with the nucleus insertion rule. This rule gives Mamaindé an alternate strategy in dealing with certain unsyllabified strings. Chapter 2 discussed how secondary licensing does not allow [+cont] segments in the coda position; such segments are left unsyllabified. After the next affixation process, however, Mamaindé has several options. One is to spread the unsyllabified coda segment to the onset position of the following syllable, such as the form in (105), where the unsyllabified /h/ coalesces with the /tx/ onset of the next syllable, forming a pre-aspirated alveolor flap, /R/.

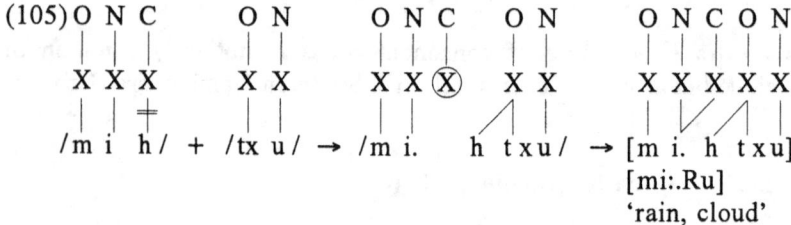

[mi:.Ru]
'rain, cloud'

An alternate strategy mentioned in chapter 2 is the insertion of a vowel, or as it is depicted here initially, a new nucleus position, between the unsyllabified coda segment and the following onset. Basically, this nucleus insertion strategy now permits the natural syllabification process to build an onset position for the /h/, thus allowing the segmental material to be syllabified easily; note (106).

(106)
```
O N C     O N    O N C N O N       O N C O N O N
| | |     | |    | | | | | |       | | | | | | |
X X X     X X    X X Ⓧ Ⓧ X X       X X X X Ⓧ X X
| |       | |    | |       | |     | |   | |   | |
/m i h/ + /tx u/ → /mi. h    tx u/ → [mi. h    tx u]
```

I call this the nucleus insertion rule. Since either of the above strategies can be used on the same form, the nucleus insertion rule below must be seen as an optional rule. It is diagrammed in (107).

(107) **Rule 7. Nucleus insertion rule** (optional) (NI)

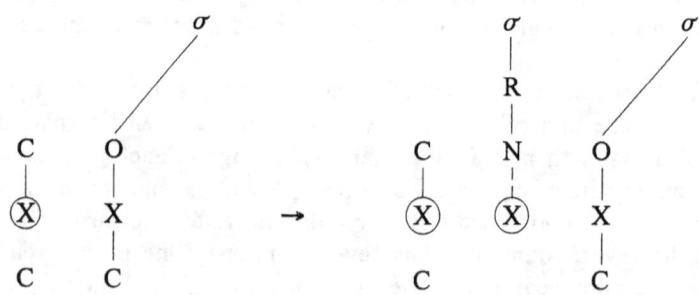

A Lexical Analysis of Mamaindé Stress

The first X in (107) is circled to signify that it has previously become orphaned and unassociated to the segmental tier.

Rule 7 inserts a nucleus position between an unsyllabified coda consonant and the following onset position. This means that in the environment of the application of this rule, the coda consonant of the first syllable must not be licensed by any licenser, but must be previously unassociated to syllable structure. Otherwise, this rule cannot apply. Notice also that this rule inserts only a nucleus and a skeletal position; no segmental features have been specified for this skeletal position yet.

After the new nucleus and skeletal position have been inserted, they must eventually be associated to the segmental tier or be deleted. This can happen in one of two ways; either by the vowel spreading rule, or by the insert [a] rule. The first rule allows the orphaned skeletal position to take its features from the closest vowel on its left; note (108).

(108) **Rule 8. Vowel spreading rule** (VS)

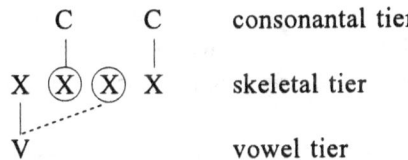

Here the circled X to which the association is made is the orphaned skeletal position that was inserted by the nucleus insertion rule above.

By separating the segmental tier into two tiers, one for consonants and one for vowels, we can see the logical target for this spreading rule. In essence, all of the features of the vowel on the left are spreading to the next available skeletal position on its right.

This spreading of features is demonstrated in the form in (109).

(109)
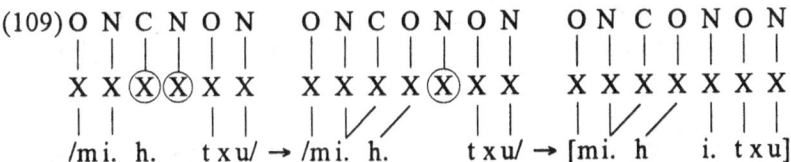

Thus the inserted nucleus borrows its features from the vowel on its left and is realized as [i]. However, if there is no vowel to the left of the inserted nucleus, as seen in the word /n.la.tha.wa/ 'it is' below in (112), this vowel spreading rule cannot apply. The features of this nucleus position will then be determined by the insert [a] rule in (110).

(110) **Rule 9. Insert [a] rule (Ia)**

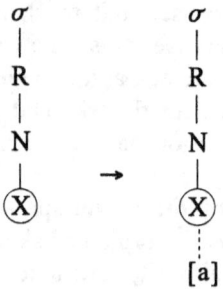

This rule inserts the vowel [a] and associates it to a nucleus position which is unassociated to any segmental material.

Since rule 9 is much broader in scope than the vowel spreading rule above, it must be ordered later by the elsewhere condition. The end result is that the insert [a] rule will apply only if the vowel spreading rule cannot apply.[30]

The insert [a] Rule can be demonstrated in the following derivation, when the pro-verb [na] 'to be' is used as the root of a word. The root [na] 'to be, to say', although very frequent, is unique in that it is the only root that never receives stress. According to Kingston (1991b), it is often semantically empty, apparently used only as a string to which affixes may attach. In fact, in normal speech, it is entirely reduced to a nasalized onset of the following syllable; the only time the [a] is pronounced is in slow, deliberate speech. This gives phonetic evidence to posit that this morpheme is underlyingly only a single nasal segment, n, and not initially part of any syllable structure, since syllables require the nucleus position to be filled. The [a] is later inserted only in slow speech by the nucleus insertion and insert [a] rules. I list this morpheme in the lexicon as shown in (111).

---

[30]If underspecification theory were being used, this insert [a] rule would probably be unnecessary, for by considering [a] as the radically underspecified vowel in Mamaindé, it would naturally follow that any vowel left underspecified would eventually get its redundant features filled in whenever full specification was carried out. These redundant features would be the complete set of distinctive features which make up the underspecified vowel [a]. As mentioned earlier, however, the underspecification of features in Mamaindé has not yet been totally worked out.

A Lexical Analysis of Mamaindé Stress   85

(111)   *n* — 'to be, to say'

This interpretation of [na] as *n* explains the reason why this root is never stressed; it consists only of a single consonant, which cannot be syllabified by itself during the first cycle of stratum I since it lacks a nucleus. Without being associated to syllabic structure and licensers, this segment cannot license a mora position on the metrical grid, and thus further stress grid marks cannot be built upon it.

When we combine this root *n* 'to be' with a string of syllables from stratum IV, such as [latha][∅][wa] (third person, present tense, declarative mood), the output of the lexical component will produce a totally unstressed form (*n* is not stressed because it lacks a nucleus, and the other morphemes are not stressed because they belong to stratum IV, where stress is not operative). However, these unstressed forms are considered unacceptable in Mamaindé since every well-formed word must have at least one stressed syllable. Thus, the reason for the presence of the ERIF rule in the postlexical component is apparent; it stresses these strings which have bypassed all the other stress rules, finally allowing them to at least partially conform to the image of a well-formed Mamaindé word. Notice also that the nucleus insertion rule must apply after the ERIF rule in order for the first syllable [na] of the surface form [na.'la.tha.wa] to remain unstressed.

Given below in (112) is a full derivation of such a word, showing how stress is finally applied to these forms via the ERIF rule and how the nucleus insertion rule and the insert [a] rule work to fill in the missing vowel (I use an upper case *V* to represent an inserted nucleus position without features).

(112) [na.'la.tha.wa] 'it is'

    LEXICAL COMPONENT   /n/ /latha/ /∅/ /wa/
    Stratum I
    Cycle 1
       affixation
          root [n]
       rules
          QS N/A
          ERFF N/A
          ERFW N/A
    Stratum II N/A
    Stratum III N/A

Stratum IV
Cycle 1
   affixation
                     x x
      subject [[n][latha]]
   rules
      no rules in this stratum
        x x
  BE [nlatha]
Cycle 2
   affixation
                   x x
      tense [[nlatha][∅]]
   rules
      no rules in this stratum
        x x
  BE [nlatha∅]
Cycle 3
   affixation
                   x x   x
      mood [[nlatha∅][wa]]
   rules
      no rules inthis stratum
       x x   x
  BE [nlatha∅wa]

POSTLEXICAL COMPONENT
   rules
              x
           x x x
   ERIF [nlathawa]
   Vowel lengthening 2   N/A
   Coda lengthening   N/A
                   x
                x x x x
   Nucleus insertion [nVlathawa]
   Vowel spreading   N/A
               x
          x x x x
   Insert [a] rule [nalathawa]

OUTPUT OF PHONOLOGY

```
            x
         x x x x
       [nalathawa]
```

Notice that if the nucleus insertion rule had applied anytime before the ERIF rule, the syllable [na] would have received stress. If the [a] had been present during the first stratum of the phonology, ERFF and ERFW would have applied word-level stress to [na]; if the [a] had been inserted any time after the first stratum of the lexical component and before the ERIF rule of the postlexical component, the lexical stress rules would not have applied any stress to the word at all and then the ERIF rule would have applied foot stress to the first syllable, [na]. Thus, the only possible explanation for the way stress has been applied to this form is for the [a] vowel not to be present until after the ERIF rule of the postlexical component has had a chance to apply. Only then can it avoid being stressed.

Note that it is possible to look at the nucleus insertion rule as a rule breaking up a consonant cluster at the beginning of a syllable which violates the SONORITY PRINCIPLE. The sonority principle, which has its origins in Bloomfield's *Language* (1933), is quoted here from Goldsmith (1990:110), and states that "segmental material in the onset of the syllable must be arranged in a linear order of increasing sonority from the beginning of the syllable to the nucleus."

Likewise, the mirror image must be true in the coda position. Thus, in Mamaindé, onsets such as [kw] are allowed but not [wk]. Mamaindé codas, on the other hand, seem to be allowed to violate this principle quite regularly (although only in their phonetic form): [yaign] 'food', [waubm] 'red'. It appears, therefore, that the sonority principle is limited to the onset position in Mamaindé, and even then it is only a weak tendency since nucleus insertion is an optional rule. The reason it is operative only in slow speech is presumably because this is precisely when the boundaries between onset, nucleus, and coda are most easily distinguished. In fast speech, the nucleus is not inserted and the nasal element in [nkhatox] coalesces with the onset segment [kh], thus becoming a single onset position, [nkh], which has been prenasalized.

The most relevant point of this nucleus insertion rule to our discussion of stress, however, is not its motivation but its interaction with the stress rules. By placing the NI rule in the postlexical component after the ERIF rule, it follows all the stress rules of the language. This means that the inserted nucleus can never be stressed, even when it occurs as the nucleus of a monosyllabic root. And this is exactly the case, as seen in the derivation of the word [na'lathawa] in (112) above.

Here, in the final part of the postlexical component I include two rules from Kingston ("Mamaindé Syllables"), which operate on the phrase level. Although phrase-level stress is not the focus of this paper, these rules could be analyzed as altering certain stress grids which were built at the foot and word levels by adding an additional phrase row to the grid. I will not argue for or against these phrase level rules, although they appear to be sound. For purposes of this presentation, these rules in (113)–(114) are translated into metrical terms.

(113) **Rule 10.** The last syllable of a clause receives one more x on its stress grid.

(114) **Rule 11.** The last stressed syllable in the sentence receives one more x on its stress grid.

I do not attempt to discuss these two phrase-level rules since they are fairly self-explanatory and my analysis focuses on those elements of stress below the phrase level.

Kingston included another rule in his phrase-level rules which pertained to those syllables which carry inherent stress, such as *yex* 'surely' and *áx* 'not'. His rule, translated into metrical terms, would basically read: To any emphatic or negative morpheme, add an extra x at the phrase level of its metrical grid column.

However, rules in the postlexical component would be blind to any internal morpheme boundaries and unaware of which syllable was actually an emphatic or negative morpheme. Therefore, a postlexical rule cannot be written to account for this emphatic stress. The only solution, as I mentioned in chapter 4, is that these few inherently stressed morphemes would have to be pre-associated to a phrase-level column of grid marks in their underlying form. Thus, the emphatic morpheme *yex* must be marked within the lexicon as shown in (115).

(115) p   x
 w   x
 f   x
 m   x
     |
  /yex/ 'surely'

Notice that this requires positing one more level or row to the metrical grid, which I label *p* for phrase level. The possibility of needing more than three layers on the metrical grid was foreseen by Goldsmith (1990:191). It should also be noted that these inherently stressed morphemes, in particular the negative morpheme *áx*, often cause stress to shift in peculiar ways. This may be due to some stress clash rule which is somehow limited to these inherently stressed morphemes. Such a rule has not been completely worked out yet and requires further study.

Keep in mind that all of the rules proposed in this section are subject to the constraints of lexical theory, applying only within their specified component or stratum.

Listed below in (116) are the strata of Mamaindé phonology with the individual stress rules combined with all of the structure-changing rules given in this chapter and in chapter 2.

(116) Mamaindé stress rules and syllable structure rules combined with the lexical strata[31]

    LEXICAL COMPONENT
    Stratum I
        Affixation processes
        Cycles
            1. stem only
            2. prefixes (including reduplicated prefixes)
            3. infixes (from reduplication)
            4. compounds

        Phonological rules
            Syllabification (including maximal onset rule)
            Vowel lengthening 1 (VL-1)
            Quantity sensitive (QS)
            End rule [final, foot] (ERFF)
            End rule [final, word] (ERFW)

---

[31]The exact ordering of specific cycles within certain strata is arbitrary in some cases. At times there is no evidence to suggest which affix attaches before another, for many of them apply in mutually exclusive environments. What is not arbitrary, however, is the grouping of these affixation processes into strata, and the subsequent ordering of these strata.

Stratum II
    Affixation processes
    Cycles
        1. auxiliary suffixes
        2. prepositions
        3. object markers
    Phonological rules
        Syllabification (including maximal onset rule)
        Vowel lengthening 1 (VL-1)
        Quantity sensitive (QS)
        End rule [final, word] (ERFW)

Stratum III
    Affixation processes
    Cycles:
        1. modifiers
        2. noun classifiers
        3. conjunctions/connectives
    Phonological rules
        Syllabification (including maximal onset rule)
        Vowel lengthening 1 (VL-1)
        Quantity sensitive (QS)

Stratum IV
    Affixation processes
    Cycles
        1. subject markers
        2. tense markers
        3. mood markers
        4. articles
    Phonological rules
        Syllabification (including maximal onset rule)
        Vowel lengthening 1 (VL-1)
            no stress rules in this stratum

A Lexical Analysis of Mamaindé Stress

POSTLEXICAL COMPONENT
    Phonological rules
        End rule [initial, foot] (ERIF)
        Vowel lengthening 2 (VL-2)
        Coda lengthening rule (CL)
        Nucleus insertion rule (NI)
        Vowel spreading rule (VS)
        Insert [a] rule (Ia)
        Phrase level stress rules

OUTPUT OF PHONOLOGY

9
Derivations

This chapter discusses the application of the above analysis to various types of forms to see how the rules and strata interact together to produce the correct output. Metrical grids are used to indicate stress placement (the use of metrical trees are reconsidered in the next chapter).

Root morphemes are indicated by small capital letters in the initial surface form. Recall that the mora row of the metrical grid is filled in for each morpheme when it is affixed to the string. This is not due to any stress rule, but rather, this mora assignment is the direct result of the principles of metrical phonology and syllabic licensing. Extra length is shown by a colon (:) on both vowels and consonants. Again, N/A can refer to a specific rule which does not apply or to a complete stratum which does not apply to a given form. It is important to keep in mind that certain phonetic details unrelated to stress are ignored in these derivations.

(117) Abbreviations of rules used

    VL-1   Vowel lengthening rule 1
    QS   Quantity sensitive rule
    ERFF   End rule [final, foot]
    ERFW End rule [final, word]
    ERIF   End rule [initial, foot]
    VL-2   Vowel lengthening rule 2
    CL   Coda lengthening
    NI   Nucleus insertion rule
    VS   Vowel spreading rule
    Ia   Insert [a] rule

First, take a look at the form in (118) which has two heavy syllables in the root. This will show that the ERFW rule does indeed stress the right-most heavy syllable in Stratum I, and that the QS rule is not operative in Stratum IV.

(118) Surface form: ′SUX.″TON:.ta.′let.nan.wa 'it wasn't known to me'

    LEXICAL COMPONENT   /suxton/ /ta/ /let/ /∅/ /nan/ /wa/

Stratum I
Cycle 1
    affixation

                           xx xx
        root   [suxton]

    rules

                           x x
                          xx xx
        QS   [suxton]

        ERFF   N/A

                           x
                         x x
                         xx xx
        ERFW   [suxton]

Derivations

Stratum II
Cycle 3
  affixation

```
                              x
                             x x
                            xx xx   x
```
        object marker   [[suxton][ta]]

  rules
      QS   N/A

      ERFW   N/A

```
                              x
                             x x
                            xx xx x
```
    BE (Bracket erasure) [suxtonta]

Stratum III
Cycle 1
  affixation

```
                              x
                             x x
                            xx xx x  xx
```
        modifier   [[suxtonta][let]]

  rules

```
                              x
                             x x     x
                            xx xx x  xx
```
      QS   [[suxtonta][let]]

```
                              x
                             x x   x
                            xx xx x xx
```
      BE   [suxtontalet]

Stratum IV
Cycle 1
 affixation

```
                    x
              x  x     x
              xx xx x xx
subject marker  [[suxtontalet][Ø]]
```

 rules
  no stress rules apply at this stratum

```
                    x
              x  x     x
              xx xx x xx
BE            [suxtontaletØ]
```

Cycle 2
 affixation

```
                    x
              x  x     x
              xx xx x xx    xx
tense         [[suxtontaletØ][nan]]
```

 rules
  no stress rules apply at this stratum

```
                    x
              x  x     x
              xx xx x xx xx
BE            [suxtontaletØnan]
```

Cycle 3
 affixation

```
                    x
              x  x     x
              xx xx x xx  xx    x
mood          [[suxtontaletØnan][wa]]
```

 rules
  no stress rules apply at this stratum

Derivations 97

```
                            x
                        x   x   x
                       xx xx x xx xx x
        BE             [suxtontaletØnanwa]
```

Output of lexical component, with final results of syllabification process

```
                            x
                        x   x   x
                       xx  xx x xx xx  x
                       [sux.ton.ta.let.nan.wa]
```

POSTLEXICAL COMPONENT

rules
    ERIF   N/A

    VL-2   N/A

```
                            x
                        x   x    x
                       xx  xx x xx xx  x
        CL             [sux.ton:.ta.let.nan.wa]
```

    NI   N/A

    VS   N/A

    Ia   N/A

OUTPUT OF PHONOLOGY

```
                            x
                        x   x    x
                       xx  xx x xx xx  x
                       [sux.ton:.ta.let.nan.wa]
```

As can be seen, these strata and their rules produce the correct output, with evidence of foot- and word-level stress applying in stratum I, only foot-level stress applying in stratum III, and no stress rules at all applying in stratum IV (otherwise the heavy syllable /nan/ would be stressed).

Additional support for stratum IV can be found in rapid speech styles. The person/tense/mood suffixes are often reduced or contracted to one almost imperceptible, devoiced syllable; at times they are completely deleted. This type of massive devoicing would seem to occur more naturally on morphemes which have no stress specifications.

In regard to metrical grids, in derivations of Mamaindé words, metrical grids are allowed to be passed from cycle to cycle (and stratum to stratum) with full specification of stress kept intact. In subsequent cycles or strata, any stress rules fill in the metrical grid for those segments that are unspecified for stress, without affecting previous grid marks. This process of "copying" grids from previous cycles is what allows the Mamaindé stress rules to make the right predictions. Halle and Vergnaud (1987), on the other hand, have suggested limiting grid copying by requiring that "cyclic affixes obliterate stresses assigned on earlier passes through the cyclic rules" (p. 93), and have used English stress rules as an example of this restriction. In English, word-level stresses are copied to subsequent cycles but secondary stresses are never copied. Mamaindé, however, seems to have no such restrictions. (Chung's 1983 analysis of stress in Chamorro seems to be closer to Mamaindé full grid copying.) I therefore conclude that Mamaindé allows the full copying of metrical grids from cycle to cycle, and from stratum to stratum. This language, then, requires a slight change in metrical theory, at least in the version espoused by Halle and Vergnaud. What seems to be missing in the theory is an additional parameter which could specify whether or not a particular language allows full grid copying or not. In Mamaindé this extra parameter would be set as in (119).

(119) Full grid copying: [yes]

Now consider the derivation of a word in (120) whose root has no heavy syllables in its underlying form. This shows how the ERFF rule applies to these forms in the absence of the QS rule.

Derivations   99

(120) Surface form [TA."NU:.ta.kha.'tox] 'give to me, then...'

    LEXICAL COMPONENT   /tanu/ /ta/ /khatox/

    Stratum I
    Cycle 1
      affixation

```
                                        x x
              root                     [tanu]

           rules
              QS                        N/A

                                         x
                                        x x
              ERFF                     [tanu]

                                         x
                                         x
                                        x x
              ERFW                     [tanu]
```

    Stratum II
    Cycle 1
      affixation

```
                                         x
                                         x
                                        x x x
         object marker                [[tanu][ta]]

           rules
              QS                        N/A

              ERFW                      N/A

                                         x
                                         x
                                        x x x
              BE                       [tanuta]
```

Stratum III
Cycle 1
affixation

```
                            x
                            x
                          x x x    x xx
     connectives       [[tanuta][khatox]]
```

rules

```
                            x
                            x      x
                          x x x    x xx
     QS                [[tanuta][khatox]]


                            x
                            x      x
                          x x x   x xx
     BE                 [tanutakhatox]
```

Stratum IV
N/A

Output of lexical component, with final results of syllabification process

```
                            x
                            x      x
                          x x x   x xx
                       [ta.nu.ta.kha.tox]
```

POSTLEXICAL COMPONENT

rules
   ERIF   N/A

```
                            x
                            x      x
                          x x x   x xx
     VL-2              [ta.nu:.ta.kha.tox]
```

Derivations

          CL   N/A

          NI   N/A

          VS   N/A

          Ia   N/A

Mora correction

```
                    x
                    x        x
                 x  xx x   x  xx
                 [ta.nu:.ta.kha.tox]
```

OUTPUT OF PHONOLOGY

```
                    x
                    x        x
                 x  xx x   x  xx
                 [ta.nu:.ta.kha.tox]
```

Notice the use of a process called MORA CORRECTION in the postlexical component of the derivation above. I do not see this as really a rule but as an automatic process which tidies up the loose ends left by syllabification and the vowel lengthening rules. The only reason it is included here is to clarify why there has been an extra grid mark added to the mora row at the very end of the above derivation. As discussed earlier, resyllabification and vowel lengthening can change the hierarchical structure of a given form, adding or deleting licensers. Mora correction, then, is the manner by which this change in the number of licensers is reflected through a parallel change in the associations to the mora row of the metrical grid. Mora correction can work two ways; first, the addition of an extra coda position must license an additional mora as in (121).

```
(121)     x               x               x
          x               x               x
          x               x               xx
        /tanu/    →     /tanu:/    →    /tanu:/
```

In the same way, any mora which becomes disassociated from its licenser (e.g., by maximization of onset), and remains unassociated at the end of the phonology, must be deleted as shown in (122).

(122)
```
      x                      x                      x
    x   x                  x   x                  x   x
  xx x xx x    x         xx x xx x   x          xx x  x x   x
  /tai:.i.yah.a.nxi/  →  /tai:.i.ya.ha.nxi/  →  /tai:.i.ya.ha.nxi/
```

Both of these functions are accomplished through the mora correction process, which could also be seen as an extra part of the syllabification task. It does not, however, affect stress placement in any way because the stress rules have already been applied. Mora correction is therefore a final attempt by the prosodic structure to align itself with the surface form, and to make sure the metrical conventions are accurately portraying the change in the number of licensers.

Before going on, a possible theoretical problem must be considered. An important aspect of all the derivations in this paper is that the first cycle of the first stratum must be limited to the root morpheme alone. This may appear to contradict the STRICT CYCLICITY condition mentioned earlier in the chapter on lexical theory. To reiterate, this condition states that "a lexical rule will not change a feature value in a non-derived context" (Goldsmith 1990:245). This would appear to prohibit any stress rules from applying to the root morpheme alone, which is obviously not a derived environment. Others phrase the notion of strict cyclicity a bit differently, stating that lexical rules should not apply to forms "which were fully present in a previous cycle" (Mohanan 1986:52). Whether this refers to forms that were fully present in the lexicon is not clear. However, as I pointed out in chapter 7, I believe that the major purpose of this strict cyclicity condition is to keep phonological rules in a particular stratum from applying to a form if some morphological material within that stratum did not apply. If my interpretation of this principle is correct, then the idea of applying Stratum I stress rules to single root morphemes in Stratum 1 is not a problem for the theory, since the root morphemes are the new morphological material that is being considered for stress in the first cycle of Stratum I. To put it another way, I believe that Stratum I phonology should be allowed to apply to Stratum I morphology.

Goldsmith (1990:222–23, 241) also points out that this strict cyclicity condition holds only for rules which change structure or features, and not to rules which simply fill in features. Exactly which of these types actually describes the Mamaindé stress rules I am not sure, but it would seem that these rules could be viewed as simply filling in metrical grids which are initially unspecified. One thing I am sure of, however, is that each derivation in this language requires that the first cycle focus only

Derivations

on the underived root. This is the only way to ensure that every root receives word-level stress, particularly those roots composed of only light syllables. For example, if the first cycle in the derivation in (120) above was forced to include a derived form, the stress rules would have to begin by considering [[tanu][ta]] as the first domain to which they could apply. The outcome would then be as in (123).

(123) **Stratum I**
Cycle 1
affixation

```
                     x x   x
                    [[tanu][ta]]

    QS               N/A

                             x
                     x x   x
    ERFF            [[tanu][ta]]

                             x
                             x
                     x x   x
    ERFW            [[tanu][ta]] *
```

This type of rule application results in an incorrect form (and would do so in almost all cases where the roots lack any heavy syllables); the stress in the above example should fall on the last syllable of the root and not on the following affix. Only by restricting the first cycle to root morphemes alone will the stress rules be able to capture a basic generalization in this language, namely, that roots must receive word-level stress.

The Mamaindé data, then, proves that in at least some languages, the very first cycle must be allowed to apply to an underived form. Intuitively this would seem to hold true for many languages, i.e., that the root is somehow treated in a special way, marked as semantically more loaded than the affixes which attach themselves to it. If this idea of applying first cycle rules to underived forms does constitute a change in the theory of lexical phonology, it is a minor one which can be carried out without affecting the rest of the theory. What should be noted, however, is that for some languages, including Mamaindé, this pattern of rule application is absolutely necessary, whether it is a theoretical innovation or not.

The next two derivations, (124)–(125), are interesting because they are words which have more than one word-level stress.

(124) Surface form *"wʌ:."he:.ni.'ya.ha.nxi* 'the exact time of coming'

    LEXICAL COMPONENT /wa/ /hen/ /iyah/ /anxi/
    Stratum I
    Cycle 1
      affixation

                            x
        root   [wa]

      rules
        QS   N/A

                            x
                          x
        ERFF   [wa]

                            x
                          x
                          x
        ERFW   [wa]

    Stratum II
    Cycle 1
      affixation

                            x
                          x
                          x xx
      auxiliary suffix [[wa][hen]]
      rules
                          x
                          x x
                          x xx
        QS   [[wa][hen]]

Derivations 105

```
                          x  x
                          x  x
                          x  xx
        ERFW           [[wa][hen]]


                           x x
                           x x
                           x xx
        BE              [wahen]
```

Stratum III
Cycle 1
affixation
```
                          x x
                          x x
                          x xx x xx
        modifier       [[wahen][iyah]]
```
rules
```
                           x x
                           x x    x
                           x xx x xx
        QS             [[wahen][iyah]]


                           x x
                           x x   x
                           x xxx xx
        BE              [waheniyah]
```

Stratum IV
Cycle 4
affixation
```
                          x x
                          x x   x
                          x xxx xx x  x
        article       [[waheniyah][anxi]]
```

rules
    no stress rules apply at this stratum

```
                        x  x
                        x  x    x
                        x xxx xxx  x
     BE                 [waheniyahanxi]
```

Output of lexical component, with final results of the syllabification process and VL-1 rule

```
                        x  x
                        x  x       x
                        x xx x xx x   x
                        [wa.he:.ni.ya.ha.nxi]
```

POSTLEXICAL COMPONENT

rules
  ERIF   N/A

```
                        x  x
                        x  x       x
                        x xx x xx x   x
  VL-2                  [wa:.he:.ni.ya.ha.nxi]
```

  CL   N/A

  NI   N/A

  VS   N/A

  Ia   N/A

Mora correction
```
                        x  x
                        x  x    x
                        xx xx x x  x   x
                        [wa:.he:.ni.ya.ha.nxi]
```

Derivations

OUTPUT OF PHONOLOGY

```
               x  x
               x  x  x
              xx xx x x  x  x
         [wa:.he:.ni.ya.ha.nxi]
```

Notice that in these derivations I am only showing the results of syllabification and the vowel lengthening 1 rule as the word leaves the lexical component. This is because of the inordinate amount of space it would take to show every detail of the syllabification process, which is crucial to the application of the VL-1 rule. As mentioned earlier, however, my own view is that the process of building syllable structure is persistant, actually occurring after each affix is added throughout the lexical component, since lexical rules such as QS must be able to refer to such hierarchical units as branching rhymes. Likewise, the VL-1 rule applies in every stratum, immediately following the syllabification process, whenever its structural description is met. In the derivations, however, I have chosen to show these processes only once. This greatly reduces the length of the diagrammed derivations and the end result is the same; each word is completely syllabified before it leaves the lexical component and the correct vowels are lengthened. (There are times, however, when further syllabification is needed in the postlexical component as well.)

The form in (125), aside from having two word-level stresses, also shows how the ERIF rule is invoked in the postlexical component to assign secondary stress to the first syllable of a string which has two unstressed syllables word initially. This rule explains why prefixes carry secondary stress, if and only if the next syllable is not stressed. This phenomenon is discussed further in chapter 11 on well-formedness statements.

(125) Surface form ′i.KA.″LA:.″ku:.′htex.na.′tax   'to work with'

    LEXICAL COMPONENT   /kala/ /i/ /kuh/ /texnatax/

Stratum I
Cycle 1
  affixation

```
                          x x
         root            [kala]
```

rules
    QS   N/A

```
                          x
                        x x
 ERFF                   [kala]

                          x
                          x
                        x x
 ERFW                   [kala]
```

Cycle 2
  affixation

```
                            x
                            x
                        x  x x
 prefixes               [[i][kala]]
```

rules
    QS   N/A

    ERFF   N/A

    ERFW   N/A

```
                          x
                          x
                        x x x
 BE                     [ikala]
```

Stratum II
Cycle 2
  affixation

```
                          x
                          x
                        x x x   xx
 preposition            [[ikala][kuh]]
```

Derivations

    rules

```
                            x
                          x x
                      x x x   xx
   QS                 [[ikala][kuh]]


                          x   x
                          x   x
                      x x x   xx
   ERFW               [[ikala][kuh]]


                          x x
                          x x
                      x x x xx
   BE                 [ikalakuh]
```

Stratum III
Cycle 3
    affixation

```
                          x x
                          x x
                      x x x xx    xx x xx
   connectives        [[ikalakuh][texnatax]]
```

    rules

```
                          x x
                          x x   x      x
                      x x x xx    xx x xx
   QS                 [[ikalakuh][texnatax]]


                          x x
                          x x   x      x
                      x x x xx xx x xx
   BE                 [ikalakuhtexnatax]
```

Stratum IV
N/A

Output of lexical component, with the final results of the syllabification process and the VL-1 rule

```
                            x  x
                         x  x  x  x     x
                         x x x xx xx x xx
                         [i.ka.la.ku:.htex.na.tax]
```

POSTLEXICAL COMPONENT

rules

```
                            x  x
                         x  x  x  x     x
                         x x x xx xx x xx
   ERIF                  [i.ka.la.ku:.htex.na.tax]


                            x  x
                         x  x  x  x     x
                         x x x xx xx x xx
   VL-2                  [i.ka.la:.ku:.htex.na.tax]
```

CL	N/A
NI	N/A
VS	N/A
Ia	N/A

Mora correction

```
                            x  x
                         x  x  x  x     x
                         x x xx xx xx x xx
                         [i.ka.la:.ku:.htex.na.tax]
```

OUTPUT OF PHONOLOGY

```
                            x  x
                         x  x  x  x     x
                         x x xx xx xx x xx
                         [i.ka.la:.ku:.htex.na.tax]
```

Consider now the form in (126) which contains one of the emphatic morphemes, /yex/, which is pre-associated in the lexicon to a phrase-level grid column.

Derivations

(126) *"SET:.'"yex:.'let.nan.wa*   speak-surely-did-3p-past-decl
                                            'He surely did speak'

LEXICAL COMPONENT

                                            x
                                            x
                                            x
                                            x
                              /set/ /yex/ /let/ /Ø/ /nan/ /wa/

Stratum I
Cycle 1
   affixation

                                       xx
             root   [set]

   rules

                                         x
                                       xx
             QS   [set]

             ERFF   N/A

                                         x
                                       x
                                       xx
             ERFW   [set]

Stratum II
Cycle 1
   affixation

                                             x
                                      x x
                                      x x
                                    xx xx
        auxiliary suffix   [[set][yex]]

rules
    QS   N/A

    ERFW   N/A

```
                        x
                      x x
                      x x
                     xx xx
BE                  [setyex]
```

Stratum III
Cycle 1
  affixation

```
                         x
                       x x
                       x x
                      xx xx  xx
modifiers           [[setyex][let]]
```

rules

```
                         x
                       x x
                       x x  x
                      xx xx  xx
QS                  [[setyex][let]]
```

```
                         x
                       x x
                       x x x
                      xx xx xx
BE                   [setyexlet]
```

Stratum IV
Cycle 1
  affixation

```
                         x
                       x x
                       x x x
                      xx xx xx
subject marker      [[setyexlet][Ø]]
```

Derivations

    rules
       no stress rules apply at this stratum

```
                           x
                          x x
                         x x x
                        xx xx xx
BE                     [setyexletØ]
```

Cycle 2
    affixation

```
                           x
                          x x
                         x x x
                        xx xx xx    xx
tense                  [[setyexletØ][nan]]
```

    rules
       no stress rules apply at this stratum

```
                           x
                          x x
                         x x x
                        xx xx xx  xx
BE                     [setyexletØnan]
```

Cycle 3
    affixation

```
                           x
                          x x
                         x x x
                        xx xx xx  xx   x
mood                   [[setyexletØnan][wa]]
```

    rules
       no stress rules apply at this stratum

```
                          x
                      x   x
                      x   x   x
                      xx xx xx xx  x
         BE           [setyexletØnan wa]
```

Output of the lexical component, with the final results of the syllabification process

```
                          x
                      x   x
                      x   x   x
                      xx xx xx xx  x
                      [set.yex.let.nan.wa]
```

POSTLEXICAL COMPONENT

rules

    ERIF   N/A

    VL-2   N/A

```
                          x
                      x   x
                      x   x   x
                      xx  xx  xx xx   x
         CL           [set:.yex:.let.nan.wa]
```

    NI   N/A

    VS   N/A

    Ia   N/A

OUTPUT OF PHONOLOGY

```
                          x
                      x   x
                      x   x   x
                      xx  xx  xx xx   x
                      [set:.yex:.let.nan.wa]
```

Derivations 115

The word in (127) illustrates the use of the nucleus insertion rule.

(127) ["mi:.hi.txu]   'a cloud, rain'

LEXICAL COMPONENT   /mih/ /txu/

Stratum I
Cycle 1
  affixation

                           xx
      root   [mih]

  rules

                            x
                            xx
      QS   [mih]

      ERFF   N/A

                            x
                            x
                            xx
      ERFW   [mih]

Stratum II
N/A

Stratum III
N/A

Stratum IV
Cycle 4
  affixation

                            x
                            x
                            xx   x
      article   [[mih][txu]]

  rules
    no stress rules apply in this stratum

```
                              x
                              x
                             xx  x
   BE                       [mihtxu]
```

Output of lexical component, with final results of syllabification process and the VL-1 rule[32]

```
                              x
                              x
                             xx   x
                            [mi:.h.txu]
```

POSTLEXICAL COMPONENT

rules

    ERIF   N/A

    VL-2   N/A

```
                              x
                              x
                             xx  x    x
   NI                       [mi:.hV.txu][33]
```

```
                              x
                              x
                             xx  x   x
   VS                       [mi:.hi.txu]
```

    Ia   N/A

---

[32]Although it may appear that the /h/ has been syllabified as a separate syllable, it actually is not syllabified here. It has become dissassociated from the coda position by the restrictions of coda licensing and has not yet been incorporated into any syllable.

[33]V is used here to represent the inserted nucleus position.

Derivations   117

    OUTPUT OF PHONOLOGY

                                    x
                                    x
                              xx x   x
                              [mi:.hi.txu]

The form in (127) above not only shows the insertion of the nucleus by the NI rule, but it also demonstrates how this inserted nucleus can get its features from the previous vowel by the VS rule.

At other times this inserted nucleus has its features filled in only by the insert [a] rule, as in the word below in (128).

(128) [na.kha.'tox]   'then'

    LEXICAL COMPONENT   /n/ /khatox/

    Stratum I
    Cycle 1
      affixation
        root   [n]

      rules
        QS   N/A

        ERFF   N/A

        ERFW   N/A

    Stratum II
    N/A

    Stratum III
    Cycle 3
      affixation
                                x xx
        conjunction   [[n][khatox]]

      rules
                                x
                              x xx
        QS   [[n][khatox]]

	x
	x xx
BE	[nkhatox]

Stratum IV
N/A

Output of lexical component, with the final results of the syllabification process

$$\begin{array}{c} x \\ x\ xx \\ [\text{n.kha.tox}]^{34} \end{array}$$

POSTLEXICAL COMPONENT
 rules

ERIF	N/A
VL-2	N/A
CL	N/A
NI	x x x xx [nV.kha.tox]
VS	N/A
Ia	x x x xx [na.kha.tox]

OUTPUT OF PHONOLOGY

$$\begin{array}{c} x \\ x\ \ x\ \ xx \\ [\text{na.kha.tox}] \end{array}$$

Finally, consider the word in (129) with a compound stem.

---
[34] At this point /n/ is not yet syllabified.

Derivations   119

(129) [TU."XAI.kha.'tox]   'grab (something) and go, then'

    LEXICAL COMPONENT   [xai] [tu] [khatox]

Stratum I
Cycle 1
   affixation

                              x
      root   [xai]

   rules
      QS   N/A

                              x
                              x
      ERFF   [xai]

                              x
                              x
                              x
      ERFW   [xai]

Cycle 4
   affixation

                                  x
                                  x
                             x x
      compounds   [[tu][xai]]

   rules
      QS   N/A
      ERFF   N/A
      ERFW   N/A

                                x
                                x
                             x x
      BE   [tuxai]

Stratum II
N/A

Stratum III
Cycle 3
   affixation

```
                              x
                              x
                          x x     x xx
      connective       [[tuxai][khatox]]
```

   rules

```
                              x
                              x   x
                          x x     x xx
      QS               [[tuxai][khatox]]


                              x
                              x   x
                          x x     x xx
      BE                [tuxaikhatox]
```

Stratum IV
N/A

Output of lexical component, with the results of the syllabification process

```
                              x
                              x   x
                          x x     x xx
                        [tu.xai.kha.tox]
```

POSTLEXICAL COMPONENT

   rules
      ERIF   N/A

```
                              x
                              x   x
                          x x     x xx
      VL-2            [tu.xai:.kha.tox]
```

Derivations   121

                    CL   N/A
                    NI   N/A
                    VS   N/A
                    Ia   N/A

        Mora correction
                                        x
                                        x   x
                                    x x x   x xx
                                [tu.xai:.kha.tox]

        OUTPUT OF PHONOLOGY
                                        x
                                        x   x
                                    x x x   x xx
                                [tu.xai:.kha.tox]³⁵

---

[35] This form undergoes an additional phonetic change due to a contraction process which has become the unmarked form of this word. The original root forms were probably linked by a connective, like this: /tu-tax-xai/ 'get-and-go'. But for present day speakers, these three syllables have become permanently fused into two, /tu−tai/. So the surface form of this word actually becomes:

            x
            x   x
        x x x   x xx
        [tu.tai:.kha.tox]

10
Metrical Trees versus Metrical Grids

10.1. Practical considerations. In this section I will argue for the superiority of the metrical grid approach over the arboreal approach in its ability to handle the Mamaindé data. I have already shown how grid theory can account for the vast majority of the data by simply setting the parameters of the four grid-based rules. Now consider whether or not metrical trees can be built in as simple a manner.

Take for example the words in (130) (roots are in small capitals).

(130) [['wa][WALE"KHAN][txu]]   'your chief'
 [['i][KA"LA:][ka][kha'tox]]   'work for, then'
 [['SUX"TON][ta][latha][wa]]   'I do not know'
 [YU"HAKX]   'all'
 ['HAX"TIN]   'quickly'

First, notice that feet must be unbounded as opposed to binary, since many of these forms have sequences where there is more than one unstressed syllable between stresses. Next, they must stress heavy syllables, thus the foot rule must be quantity sensitive. By looking at the roots alone, it is evident that roots with one heavy syllable such as *walekhan* 'chief' and *yuhakx* 'all', must have right-headed feet. Directionality is not an issue for this rule since feet are unbounded.

This first arboreal foot rule is stated in (131).

(131) Arboreal foot building rule A. Construct right-headed, quantity sensitive, unbounded feet.

A second rule is needed to build foot structure for roots like /kala/ 'to work', where there are no heavy syllables. Goldsmith (1990) gives examples of languages which have these same two foot-assigning strategies as mentioned earlier. This rule is stated in (132).

(132) Arboreal foot building rule B. Construct right-headed, quantity insensitive, unbounded feet.

A word-building rule is also necessary. Because of roots like /'sux"ton/ 'not knowing', which give prominence to the right-most foot, it appears that words are right-headed. Thus, the rule in (133).

(133) Arboreal word building rule. Construct right-headed, quantity sensitive words.

Since the data includes many secondary stressed syllables, the last parameter, dealing with the suppression of secondary stress, would be stated as in (134).

(134) Secondary stress suppression: No

These rules must then be divided into strata just as the metrical rules were; note (135).

(135) Strata:

    I.   Arboreal foot building rule A
          Arboreal foot building rule B
          Arboreal word building rule

    II. Arboreal foot building rule A
          Arboreal word building rule

    III. Arboreal foot building rule A

    IV. No stress rules

Metrical Trees versus Metrical Grids

These rules work well in building prosodic structure for most forms in the first cycle of stratum I, such as *haxtin* 'quick', shown in (136).

(136) Arboreal foot building rule A

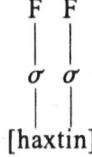

Arboreal word building rule

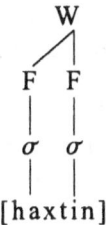

But then there are words like ["onkakha'tox] 'work, then'. In the first stratum, the three stress rules above (131)–(133) are applied to the root morpheme alone, /onka/. After building the head of a foot over /on/ because it is heavy, we must also build a foot over /ka/ because it is the right-most syllable and the foot rule tells us to build right-headed feet; note (137).

(137) F   F
       | |
       σ   σ
       | |
       [onka]

A glance at the surface form, ["onkakha'tox], however, shows that the second syllable does not receive any stress at all, and therefore the foot structure above the second syllable must be deleted. I might try positing that this is a DEGENERATE foot (one that does not contain the right number of syllables) and state that degenerate feet are not allowed in this language (Goldsmith (1990) deletes degenerate feet in his treatment of MalakMalak). However, degenerate feet are possible only when monosyllabic feet are encountered in a bounded or binary system. In unbounded systems, such as Mamaindé, the number of syllables per foot is not an issue and therefore monosyllabic feet are acceptable. This is made obvious by the presence of many monosyllabic roots like ["tu] 'get' and ["wa] 'come' which receive both foot- and word-level stress. Obviously, then, the last syllable of ["on.ka] cannot be considered a degenerate foot. Nor can the notion of extrametricality be appealed to here, since there would be no way to distinguish the last syllable of this verb from the last syllable of other verbs which do get stressed, such as [ta."nu] 'give'. The only other possible way to delete the foot-level stress above this last syllable, using the arboreal theory, would be to posit that the SUPPRESSION OF SECONDARY STRESS is active in Mamaindé. But this option was ruled out earlier when the arboreal rules were constructed, since it was noted that secondary stress is very evident throughout this language. The arboreal theory, then, seems incapable of handling this problem.

Some way must be found to delete the foot structure above the last syllable of [onka]. This stray syllable must then be joined to the syllabic structure of the word in some way or it will not appear in the surface form. This could be done through the process of STRAY SYLLABLE ADJUNCTION, which associates stray syllables to the nearest foot structure, shown by the dotted lines in (138).

(138) F
     / ˑˑ
    σ   σ
    | |
    [onka]

For all practical purposes, this solution builds a left-headed foot with a right-headed foot rule. The word building rule then applies giving us the form in (139).

(139) W
      |
      F
     / ˑˑ
    σ   σ
    | |
    [onka]

Metrical Trees versus Metrical Grids

The second stratum does not add any new structure to this form and therefore does not apply. In Stratum III the morpheme /khatox/ is added. Recall that only the arboreal foot rule A is active here. By adding the morpheme /khatox/ 'then', the foot structure in (140) is built.

(140)
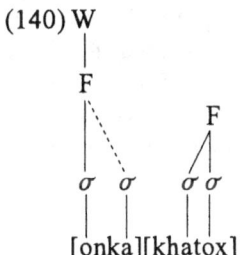

Now there is a right-headed and a left-headed foot in the same word. The only other alternative would be to delete the weak branch of the first foot (the one created by stray adjunction) and incorporate that syllable into the following foot in order to preserve the right-headed foot rule. This process is illustrated in (141).

(141)
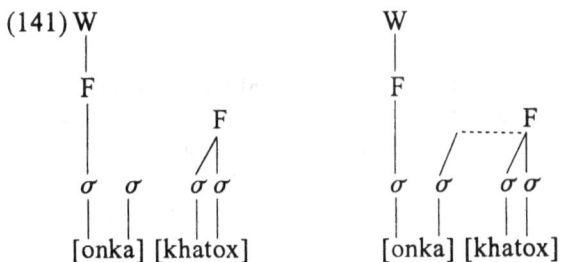

This type of deleting and reassigning of syllabic structure, however, seems only to be a way of covering up the fact that the arboreal rules are not making the right predictions. What criteria would predict which weak branches would be reassigned and which would be left alone?

To put it another way, how is it possible to syllabify these once "stray" syllables, such as /ka/ above, which are now located in the middle of a word? Metrical theory normally constrains the use of stray syllables, whether they be degenerate or extrametrical, by insisting that they occur at one end of a string. However, the fact that Mamaindé stress rules apply within several different strata creates the possibility that such degenerate or stray syllables can be found between two stressed syllables or feet, as in the word above. This seems no different than positing an extrametrical syllable in the middle of a word. Because of the way Mamaindé stress rules are spread over several strata,[36] the arboreal approach is forced to make some rather unprecedented and awkward predictions when deciding which syllable belongs to which foot.

To further complicate matters, this new foot [khatox] must be incorporated into the word structure because if it remains unattached it will be deleted. But the word-building rule is not operative in Stratum III to which [khatox] belongs, so we can not build any new word structure above this morpheme. We are therefore forced to attach this foot to the previous word structure already built, constructing a left-headed word, as in (142).

(142)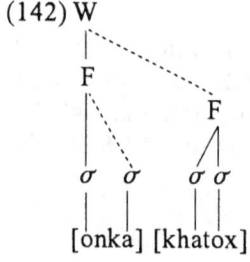

The final outcome is that both our foot-building and word-building rules have turned out to be unpredictable, sometimes building right-headed structures and at other times building left-headed structures.

A few more examples show the pervasiveness of this problem. The form in (143) has a single word level structure that is both right- and left-headed.

---

[36]The literature on metrical theory presents numerous examples of languages whose stress rules apply only at one location or within one stratum of the phonology, whether that be lexically or postlexically. Waorani is the only other language I have encountered which seems to require different stress rules for different strata. (See Lester 1994). Of course, there is nothing within the metrical theory that would keep stress rules from applying in more than one stratum. The point of the discussion here, though, is that this type of rule application can create awkward situations for the arboreal approach.

(143)   Stratum I   Stratum III

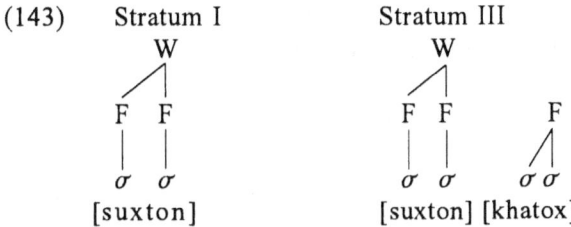

Now a process affecting feet comparable to stray syllable adjunction is the only alternative for incorporating this second morpheme into the word structure because word building rules are not available in stratum III. This is shown in (144).

(144)

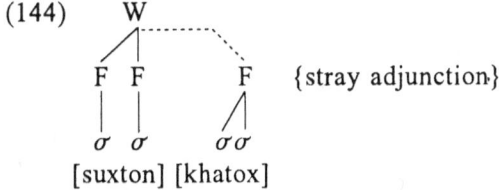   {stray adjunction}

So again the statement on word-headedness is inconsistent.

Now consider a form with a foot that is both right- and left-headed, diagrammed in (145):

(145)

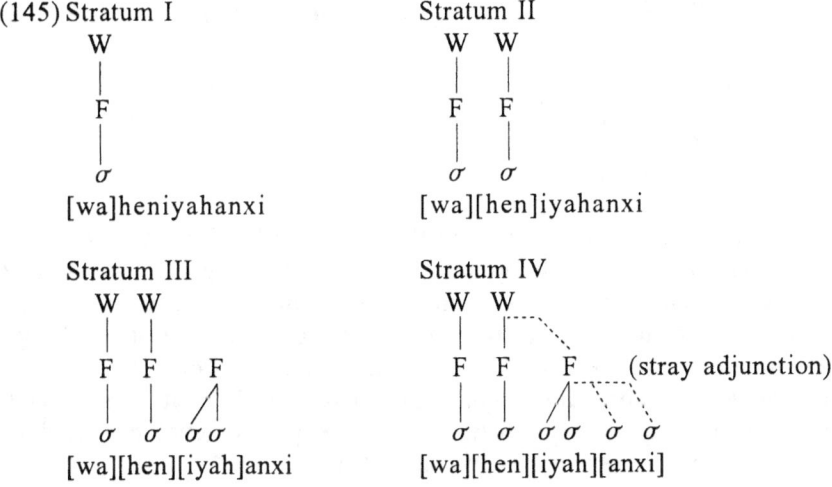

Finally, consider the form in (146) with two word-level structures, one of which is right-headed and the other left-headed.

(146)

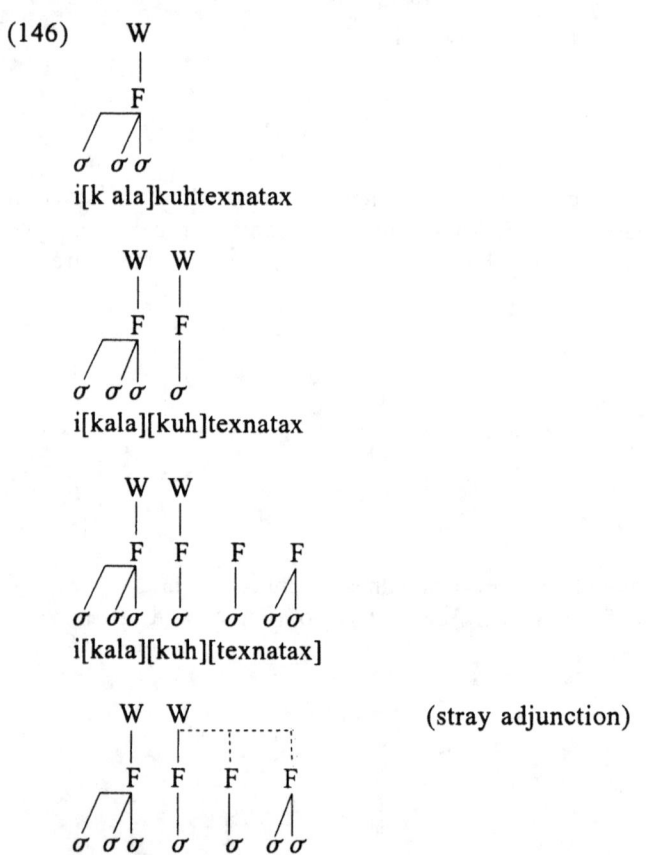

Notice that in the form in (146) the two word-level structures are not connected in any way. It appears that an arboreal approach would have to posit an additional level of structure for this language, since there would have to be a way to tie together strings with several word-level stresses into a single unit. The only way to do this would be to posit a higher level of structure that has these word levels as its constituents, perhaps the phrase: (but distinct from the phrase level proposed by Kingston and discussed above); note (147).

(147)

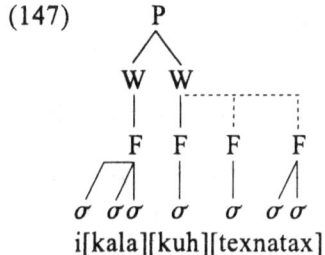

i[kala][kuh][texnatax]

The addition of a higher level structure tying together all Mamaindé words is actually intuitively appealing as this is a highly polysynthetic language where words can be composed of many morphemes and function as entire phrases would in many other languages. But for the arboreal approach, this would mean that there would have to be another level of stress in all strings with more than one word-level structure, possibly the PHRASE level, which would have to choose between the existing word structures, picking one as dominant or strong, resulting in right- or left-headed phrases. There are actually some bits of evidence in Mamaindé that when two or more word-level stresses are adjacent, one of them, the right-most one, seems to receive prominence. But this is not at all a prevalent pattern, for most of these forms appear to stress all word-level structures equally. Still, this is an option that an arboreal (or metrical) approach to Mamaindé could explore.

Whether or not this higher level exists, the arboreal rules have not captured any generalizations about prosodic structure at the foot or word level. This is due not so much to any inadequacy in the arboreal rules, but rather to the fact that the units of Mamaindé structure above the syllable are hazy, to say the least. The fact that arboreal theory emphasizes the defining of boundaries of prosodic units makes it difficult to apply to a language where all that is evident are the most pronounced points of these structures and not their internal structure. This ambiguity within Mamaindé contradicts a specific view within metrical theory known as the RECOVERABILITY CONDITION. This condition was proposed by Halle and Vergnaud (1987), and states that "given direction of government-constituent boundaries must be unambiguously recoverable from the location of the heads." As illustrated above, however, this is often impossible in Mamaindé, and for that reason the arboreal theory is not useful. The metrical grid, on the other hand, is not forced to make any reference to the boundaries of feet or words, but only to their prominent peaks.

In light of the foregoing discussion, I conclude that the arboreal theory of metrical phonology cannot be applied to Mamaindé in any consistent way that predicts stress. Therefore the grid approach must be preferred for this language, as it is totally capable of predicting stress without making mistaken inferences about the boundaries of prosodic structure.

Obviously, this translates into strong evidence for Prince's grid theory (1984), supporting the claim that it has a necessary place within metrical phonology.

10.2. Theoretical implications. Although the layered rows of metrical grids can show phonetic prominence easily, they cannot be used to extrapolate the relationships between syllables, which basically results in the inability to define constituent structure such as feet.[37] This is definitely a loss for the grid approach. This loss, however, is mostly due to the theoretical basis for metrical grids. Whereas the arboreal approach intends to be a direct representation of the internal makeup of a word, "grid theory takes the metrical grid to be an autonomous structure," separate from the string of syllables, associating to it by means of the principles of autosegmental phonology (Goldsmith 1990:193, 195). The fact that arboreal approaches to Mamaindé are not successful, and metrical grids are, suggests the strong possibility that stress in this language is more like an autosegment (like other prosodies) as grid theory would imply, than the result of a hierarchical structure. This is the position that I am taking in this paper, namely that the bottom, or mora, row of each metrical grid is associated to the skeletal tier separately from syllable structure, although it is the syllable structure which actually licenses this association. In other words, the syllable and coda positions are each allowed to license one and only one x on the mora row of the metrical grid (see also Goldsmith 1990:207). This is because "a given licenser can license no more than one occurrence of the autosegment in question" (Goldsmith 1990:123). Goldsmith's notion of licensing is one of the most compelling arguments for viewing stress as an autosegment, for he clearly has captured a striking similarity between the way syllables license metrical grids and the way they license tonal autosegments (1990:167, 170). Both tones and grids can have two licensers, the

---

[37]Halle and Vergnaud (1987), however, use the metrical grid in a way that preserves these boundaries. They use parentheses around grid marks, usually those on the mora row, to show the boundaries of each foot. Unfortunately, this explicit marking of foot structure would run into the same problems in Mamaindé as the arboreal approach has, namely, that the boundaries of these structures are not definable in this language. For that reason I have chosen not to adapt this formalism.

syllable and the coda. This explains why many tonal languages (including Mamaindé) can associate two tones to a closed syllable but only one tone to an open syllable. In the same way, many languages (those which are quantity sensitive) can associate two grid positions to closed syllables but only one grid position to open syllables. Goldsmith claims that this similarity in the behavior of tone and stress is due to the fact that they both exist independently of syllable structure, but must obey the licensing constraints that syllable structure imposes upon all prosodic features.

The idea that stress is not a product of hierarchical structure does not take away the usefulness of the arboreal approach as a means of portraying the internal make-up of syllable, foot, and word structures. It appeals to our intuition that words must be organized into smaller units in some way. I am, however, pointing out the relevance of the Mamaindé data as a language in which stress can be consistently predicted only by the grid theory, which in its weakest form would indicate that in some languages, hierarchical structure has become undefinable, at least as far as stress placement is concerned. This is because stress has become separated from structure, possibly as a result of diachronic change, functioning instead as an autosegment which can no longer serve as a means to mark the boundaries of structural units, but only their prominent peaks (see also Giegerich 1985:235).

11
Well-Formedness Statements

The preceding chapters have presented a discussion of how the entire Mamaindé stress system functions. For a broader perspective, this chapter looks at the universal processes which act as motivators for these language-specific rules. It is important to see this stress system within its larger context, which can best be described by means of statements of relative well-formedness.

The principle idea behind WELL-FORMEDNESS STATEMENTS (hereafter called WFS) is that there exists a basic universal grammar shared by all languages. This premise is based on the fact that cross-linguistically, the outputs of individual grammatical and phonological systems tend to be molded by the same kinds of principles. This universal grammar, then, consists of statements (WFS) which describe what a universally acceptable surface form would look like. If this hypothesis holds true, then all languages would feel some pressure to conform their phonological outputs to some "ideal" representation. Halle and Vergnaud (1987:280ff.) mention this higher level of universal phonological principles which motivate language specific rules in their classic study, *An Essay on Stress,* as does Goldsmith (1990:322–31).

An example of a WFS would be the sonority principle, described by Goldsmith (1990), and based upon Bloomfield's idea that all syllables demonstrate an up-and-down of sonority (Bloomfield [1933] 1984). This principle states that syllables are better formed if they contain the most sonorant element in the nucleus and then increasingly less sonorant segments towards the peripheries of the syllable. This seems to be a universal WFS, for it appears to have a strong influence across languages.

Clearly, however, not all languages conform to the sonority principle. English, for example, allows an *s* to be peripheral to seemingly less sonorant material both in the onset and coda of a syllable. Thus we can have, e.g., *strike* and *cats* which violate the sonority principle. But there is some phonetic evidence in English that this nonconforming *s* tends to lengthen and virtually create its own syllable. Compare the ability we have in slow speech to make two syllables (syllables in the phonetic sense, not in any structural sense) out of *cats* but never more than one out of *cows*. This is a small example of how a WFS may be exerting its influence in a language, even though that language is not able to fully conform to that WFS. I will posit, then, that all languages feel the pressure to conform to these universal statements of well-formedness, but not all languages have the means to fully do so. In other words, they may not have all the language specific rules necessary with which to make their surface forms identical to some universal ideal.

These language specific rules I call REPAIR STRATEGIES, a term which Goldsmith uses to refer to rules which modify or repair a form only when it violates a particular statement of well-formedness. Some of these WFS Goldsmith calls PHONOTACTICS, and he uses them to build his theory of harmonic phonology (Goldsmith 1990:322–31). However, I will not be using the term phonotactic, for I do not intend to argue here for a harmonic approach to Mamaindé stress. Although there appear to be many similarities between harmonic phonology and what I am proposing here, Goldsmith's specific presentation of harmonic phonology does not allow for different strata within the lexical component of the phonology. And, as seen in the preceding chapters, multiple strata are essential to the prediction of Mamaindé stress.

By using WFS, metrical rules such as QS and perfect grid can be seen as universal parameters which specific languages need only to turn "on" or "off." Thus, the Mamaindé child must simply acquire the rules that say "yes" to QS and "no" to perfect grid, for example. The rules of QS and PG themselves belong to universal grammar. All the language specific rules outlined in the chapters above are not simply a set of ad hoc, arbitrary rules. They are actually algorithms or repair strategies which follow directly from the WFS, and specify how the Mamaindé word is modified to conform to a particular WFS, and thus arrive closer to some universally accepted representation. The chart in (148) lists the statements which I believe are the motivating forces behind the scenes of Mamaindé stress.

Well-Formedness Statements

(148) Well-formedness statements[38]

WFS A
```
x
xx. is better formed than xx.
```

A stressed heavy syllable is better formed than an unstressed heavy syllable.

Repair strategy for WFS A: QS rule

WFS B
```
x                          x
xx. is better formed than  x.
```

A stressed heavy syllable is better formed than a stressed light syllable.

Repair strategy for WFS B: VL-1 rule
VL-2 rule

WFS C
```
x        x                         x
x.x.x or x.x.x is better formed than x.x.x or x.x.x
```

A domain of stress with peripheral foot stress is better formed than one with nonperipheral foot stress.

Repair strategy for WFS C: ER [final, foot]

WFS D
```
x        x                         x
x        x                         x
x.x.x or x.x.x is better formed than x.x.x or x.x.x
```

A domain of stress with peripheral word stress is better formed than one with nonperipheral word stress.

Repair strategy for WFS D: ER [final, word]

---

[38]Statements A and B are from Goldsmith 1990. Periods are used to indicate syllable boundaries.

WFS E
    x
    x.x is better formed than x.x

A string of two adjacent syllables with one foot level stress is better formed than a string of two adjacent syllables without any foot level stress.

Repair strategy for WFS E: ER [initial, foot]

WFS F
    CV(X). is better formed than V(X).

A syllable with onset is better formed than one without onset.

Repair strategy for WFS F: syllabification and maximal onset principle

WFS G

$$\text{.CV.CV. is better formed than} \quad .\overset{[-\text{cont}]}{\underset{[+\text{cont}]}{\overset{|}{C}\underset{|}{C}V}}.$$

Two syllables with simple onsets are better formed than one syllable with a complex onset which violates the sonority principle.

Repair strategy for WFS G: nucleus insertion.

Most of these statements and their relationships to the repair strategies are self explanatory, but note the following comments on statements C, D, and E.

The motivation for statements C and D seems to come from a need within many languages to mark the boundaries of prosodic structure. Why this seems to be a tendency is not totally clear, but it appears that processes such as the epenthesis and contraction of syllabic structure might be facilitated in languages which mark the boundaries of structural constituents in some way. Halle and Vergnaud (1987:281) argue for this same universal constraint.

Well-Formedness Statements 139

The structure of an alternating pattern of stresses is described at the higher level by positing the rule 'Construct boundaries'. At the lower level the effective construction process is described by means of a rule written in the SPE format.

Consider now WFS E. This condition would be the basis for perfect grid in most languages, basically reducing the distance between stressed elements to no more than one syllable. Kingston ("Mamaindé Syllables") has even noted a slight tendency within Mamaindé to stress every other syllable when possible.

For example, the words in (149) show a perfect grid pattern.

(149) ['i.ka."la:.ka.'tex.na.'tax]   'in order to work'
      ['wa.ha."lo:.txu]   'your land'

This is an illusory fit, however, for if the prefixes or suffixes change, the perfect grid pattern is no longer retained as shown in the forms in (150).

(150) ['i.ka."la:.ka.kha.'tox]   'work for, then'
      ['nu.sa.ha."lo:.txu]   'our land'

Notice the gaps of two adjacent unstressed syllables in the middle of both of these words. This is extremely common in Mamaindé, as is the occurrence of two adjacent stressed syllables. What is not common, however, are two (or more) adjacent unstressed syllables at the very beginning of a word. Note that all four words in (149)–(150) would pass through the stress rules of the lexical component without receiving any stress on either of the first two syllables with the result in (151).

(151) Output of lexical component

/i.ka."la:.ka.'tex.na.'tax/   'in order to work'
/wa.ha."lo:.txu/   'your land'
/i.ka."la:.ka.kha.'tox/   'work for, then'
/nu.sa.ha."lo:.txu/   'our land'

The sequence of two or more unstressed syllables at the extreme left edge of the word are apparently not tolerated in Mamaindé, for it is only in these specific situations that the end rule [initial, foot] of the postlexical component is called upon. This rule corrects the problem, always stressing the first of these unstressed syllables, and thereby causing them to comply with WFS E. Notice in (152) that two unstressed syllables in the middle of the string are not affected by this rule, although those at the beginning are.

(152) Output of the postlexical component

['i.ka."la:.ka.'tex.na.'tax]
['wa.ha."lo:.txu]
['i.ka."la:.ka.kha.'tox]
['nu.sa.ha."lo:.txu]

It is now apparent why this tendency towards perfect grid is such a limited phenomenon in Mamaindé; it is because of the repair strategy that Mamaindé has available for WFS E. In Mamaindé, this WFS is complied with only at the postlexical level, and then only by applying a limited repair strategy, the ERIF rule. Because it is postlexical, having the word as its whole domain, and because it is an end rule, the ERIF can apply stress only to the initial syllable of a word, regardless of whether there are any other sequences of two unstressed syllables in the string. This tendency, then, towards perfect grid is limited to the first two syllables of the Mamaindé word, and is accomplished not by a perfect grid rule, but by the ERIF rule which applies stress only to the first of these syllables.

Remember also that repair strategies apply only if the appropriate WFS is violated and only if the application of the rule would improve the well-formedness of the string. Thus the ERIF rule does not apply to forms such as [wa"minitxu] 'your father'. The first two syllables are not both unstressed and therefore do not violate WFS E. And although the last two adjacent syllables do violate the WFS E, the ERIF is unable to improve their form because it can affect only the first syllable of a word, and therefore it does not apply here.

The word [waha"lo:txu] 'your land', on the other hand, both violates the WFS E and also gives the ERIF repair strategy an opportunity to do something about it. Since the two adjacent unstressed syllables are located word initially, the ERIF is able to apply, adding foot level stress to the first syllable of the word. The output of the phonology is then ['waha"lo:txu]. Notice that application of this repair strategy effectively reduces the distance between stressed syllables, causing this word to be better formed in regards to the WFS E.

By using well-formedness statements, it is possible to state the ERIF rule without complicated language-specific details describing the specific environment in which it applies. This environment is already encoded in WFS E, for it is part of the universal domain of that WFS, namely, a domain consisting of two adjacent unstressed syllables. Since many languages appeal to this same type of bisyllabic domain in the application of such stress rules as perfect grid, it is redundant to specify the environment again in the Mamaindé stress rules. It is only necessary to note which universal WFS is motivating the rule, then apply the rule when, and only when, that WFS is violated.

Payne (1990) notes that Amazonian languages tend to have left-headed morphology, with the root on the left edge of the word, thus containing more suffixes than prefixes. This tendency is also prominent in Mamaindé and is evidenced by the fact that the majority of the words begin with the root morpheme, which is always marked as prominent by a primary stress. I believe this tendency is captured by the WFS E, in turn motivating the ERIF rule, which attempts to maintain this leftheadedness in words that have lost it due to prefixation or a total lack of stress. By stressing the first syllable of such words, Mamaindé continues to emphasize the prominence given to the left-most position, thereby conforming to the WFS E.

It is evident, then, that by making use of the concept of WFS within a lexical model, the motivation of the lexical rules are better explained. WFS tie the language-specific Mamaindé stress rules in with the universal notions of well-formedness that are available and active in most languages. The only difference is that in Mamaindé, although these WFS are always operative, the repair strategies which the language has at its disposal are not, and in fact they are governed or restricted by strata divisions. Thus many completed words will not be able to satisfy all the WFS. They will conform to these universals as well as possible, given the language particular constraints. Like words in most languages,

Mamaindé words travel a path which takes them as close as possible to some universal notion of well-formedness.[39]

---

[39]There are, of course, several residue areas which have not been fully accounted for in this preliminary study of Mamaindé stress. In my mind, however, none of them actually disproves any of the basic claims made here, but simply require some constraints or additions to the original hypothesis. The areas which require further study include the following:

1. The inherently stressed morphemes and the stress clash they seem to produce. An example of this can be found in the forms: [na.'sox."keuh.la.tha.wa] 'it probably is' and [na."sox.keuh.'"yex.la.tha.wa] 'it probably, most surely is'. Notice that the simple addition of the inherently stressed morpheme /'"yex/ 'surely' causes the word-level stress on the previous syllable to be deleted. However, this type of stress clash is rare and seems limited to the inherently stressed morphemes.

2. The possibility of right-headed phrase structures within Mamaindé words which contain more than one word-level stress.

3. The possibility of extra-heavy syllables.

4. The form [wa.le."khan.txu], 'chief', so far the only one of its type found, which does not follow the ERIF rule. This could mean the existence of an additional stratum for prefixes alone, where the ERIF rule is active. Forms without prefixes, then, such as the one above, would never be considered as domains for this rule.

5. The noun classifier ['thã], 'group', which is always stressed even though it is a light syllable in Stratum II, and therefore should be unstressed. Underlyingly, this may actually be a heavy syllable, /than/, which loses its coda nasal segment after stress has been assigned, and the nasal autosegment then associates to the preceding vowel.

6. The relationship between tone sandhi and stress alterations in the Mamaindé negative construction. A falling tone autosegment and a phrase-level stress autosegment seem to mark the negative. However, not only do these alterations affect the polarity of a construction, they also cause a switch in the person-hood of the subject. These complicated constructions have yet to be analyzed in a satisfactory manner. Following are some examples of the Mamaindé negative; the patterns illustrated here are consistent for most verbs. As elsewhere, tone is marked using Kingston's method (^{1} falling tone, ^{2} rising tone, ^{3} low tone, ^{4} high tone.) ["x̱ai^2.ax^3.wa^3] 'I'm going', ["x̱ai^1.ax^3.wa^3] 'he isn't going', ["x̱aidn^2.nax^3.wa^3] 'you are going', ["x̱aidn^1.nax^3.wa^3] 'I am not going'. Notice the change in both polarity and person. (The positive counterpart to the third person subject form is ["x̱ai^2.la^3.tha^3.wa^3] 'he is going'.) The most interesting form of all is the second person negative, where there is a consistent change in the location of primary stress as well as the falling tone [x̱aidn^3."na^1.ax^3.wa^3] 'you are not going'. An extra syllable is also inserted.

Appendix
A Comparative Study of Indigenous Brazilian Stress Systems

Some final questions come to mind in light of the preceding analysis with regard to other indigenous Brazilian stress systems. Many of these questions can only be completely answered after further research, but in this appendix I attempt to begin exploring the areas which merit further attention. In the preceding chapters I proposed a rather complex system to account for Mamaindé stress. How does this combination of stress rules fit in to the overall scene of indigenous Brazilian languages? Is it attested to in any of its neighbors? In particular, are there other languages in this area of the world that require a stratal approach to stress?

To provide a basis for answering these questions, I have attempted to classify a cross-section of indigenous Brazilian languages according to the stress rules they employ. At the risk of oversimplifying the data, or perhaps misunderstanding it, I have made a stress taxonomy of twenty-four languages, from twelve different language families. It is intended as a thumbnail overview of the sorts of stress systems found within Brazil. It is hoped that this taxonomy will be useful as a starting point for anyone interested in the study of stress in these or related languages, at least in the sense that the tendency of each language can be understood at a glance. In addition, I will try to determine whether or not there is any correlation between individual stress rules and particular language families.

At the outset a caveat is in order. I do not claim any personal knowledge of the languages listed here (except of course for Mamaindé). All the data used for this classification was gleaned from the results of research by others, referenced at the end of this appendix. For additional information other than that cited here on any particular language and its stress system, the reader is referred to the source indicated. Note that the languages listed here are only those for which I have been able to locate information on stress. Obviously, these twenty-four languages are only a fraction of Brazil's 200 or so indigenous languages.

In this presentation, languages are listed under each rule that applies in that language, followed by the level at which that rule applies if appropriate, e.g., foot or word level. Some additional information, such as extrametricality and directionality, is indicated where pertinent. Metrical rules are given both in grid terminology and in arboreal terminology. Languages with more than one stress rule are listed separately under each rule that applies. Any complex details in the application of these rules for particular languages are not mentioned here in order to maintain focus on the major characteristics of each language. Therefore each rule should be viewed more as an overall tendency for the languages listed in each category, and not necessarily a complete account of the stress systems in those languages.

The classifications according to language family and stock come from Rodrigues (1986), considered by many to be the leading authority on Brazil's indigenous languages. Both the family and stock classifications are given whenever possible in order to show relationships between languages. The abbreviations used are as follows:

AK	Arawak family	MK	Maku family
AN	Arawan family	MU	Mura family
CA	Carib family	NB	Nambiquára family
ER	End rule	PG	Perfect grid
GU	Guaikuru family	QS	Quantity sensitivity
JE	Je family	R-L	right-to-left
KA	Kamakan family (extinct)	TG	Tupi-Guaraní family
L-R	left-to-right	TU	Tupi stock
MA	Maxakalí family	YA	Yanomami family
MJ	Macro-Je stock		

Appendix

Classification of indigenous Brazilian languages according to stress rules

1. Quantity insensitive languages   Family

End rule (unbounded feet), [final] (right-headed)

Kayapó	At foot and word levels. Possibility for lexical strata.	JE, MJ
Kradahó	At foot and word levels. [This is a dialect of Kayapó, but is not listed in Rodrigues' book.]	JE, MJ
Asuriní	At foot and word levels. Final syllable extrametrical. Some stress seems governed by morpheme category and may profit from the application of lexical strata. Stress clash very active.	TG, TU
Uáiuái	At foot and word levels. Some final syllables extrametrical.	CA
Guajajára	At foot and word levels. Some stress seems governed by semantic factors.	TG, TU
Kamayurá	At word level. PG at foot level.	TG, TU
Urubú	At word level. PG at foot level. Appears to require lexical strata.	TG, TU
Canela	At foot and word levels.	JE, MJ

Sanumã	At foot and word levels. Also has ER [initial, foot]. Final syllable extrametrical. Stress clash active. Appears to require lexical strata. Could possibly have ternary feet.	YA
Macushi	At foot, word, and phrase levels.	CA
Wayampí	At foot and word levels.	TG, TU
Kamakan	At foot and word levels.	KA, MJ

End rule (unbounded feet), [initial] (left-headed)

Sanumã	At foot level.	YA
Kadiwéu	At foot and word levels. Appears to require lexical strata.	GU

Perfect grid (bounded, binary feet), peak first

Apinayé	R-L (right-headed) at foot level. Apparently no word level stress. Final vowel may be extrametrical.	JE, MJ
Banawá	L-R (left-headed) at foot level. Trough first, R-L at word level. Deletes all but final word level stress. Initial vowel extrametrical.	AN
Kamayurá	R-L (right-headed) at foot level. ER [final, word].	TG, TU
Urubú	R-L (right-headed) at foot level. ER [final, word]. Evidence for lexical strata.	TG, TU

Perfect grid (bounded, binary feet), trough first

Banawá	R-L (left-headed) at word level. All but final word level stress is deleted.	AN

2. Quantity sensitive languages

End rule (unbounded feet), [final] (right-headed)

Mura-Pirahã[40]
    Word level, limited to last three syllables of the word.   MU

Hixkaryána
    Foot and word levels, also has QS rule.   CA

Mamaindé   Foot and word levels, also has QS rule. Stress rules applied according to strata and morpheme category.   NB

Apalaí   Foot and word levels. Final syllable extrametrical. QS and stress clash. Secondary stress needs more study.   CA

End rule (unbounded feet), [initial] (left-headed)

Kamã   Word level, also has PG rule at foot level. Second coda segment is extrametrical.   MK

Terêna   Foot, word, and phrase levels. Uses stress for syntactic functions.   AK

---

[40]This is perhaps an overly simplified way to look at this stress system, but since primary stress always falls on the right-most heavy syllable (as long as it is one of the last three syllables), Mura-Pirahã has much in common with other languages in this grouping. For that reason I have listed it here. It is also listed under ternary grid, a term I use to accommodate the notion of ternary feet, which are required in a more detailed analysis of Mura-Pirahã stress (Everett 1988).

Mamaindé	Foot level. This rule restricted to postlexical application.	NB

Perfect grid (bounded, binary feet), peak first

Xavánte	R-L (right-headed). Word level stress not mentioned. One specific final suffix is extrametrical.	JE, MJ

Perfect grid (bounded, binary feet), trough first

Kamã	R-L (left-headed). Also uses ER [initial, word].	MK

Ternary grid (bounded, ternary feet)

Mura-Pirahã	R-L (right-headed), only right-most foot carries primary stress. One specific extrametrical syllable, word final. Also has QS rule which includes onset and voicing characteristics in its definition of heavy syllables.	MU

Quantity sensitive rule

Mura-Pirahã	MU
Nambiquára	NB
Mamaindé	NB
Hixkaryána	CA
Apalaí	CA

3. Stress operative, but apparently unpredictable

Parecís	Stress is lexically distinctive. Stress also governed by syntax.	AK

Appendix

Nambiquára
Besides the QS rule, no other stress   NB
rules have been formalized. Stress
influenced by morphological category
of morpheme. May be similar to
Mamaindé stress system but this has not
been confirmed.

4. No stress operative at all

Maxakalí   MA, MJ

5. Languages which appear to have stress rules in lexical component

Kadiwéu   GU
Xavánte   JE, MJ
Kayapó   JE, MJ
Banawá   AN
Asuriní   TG, TU
Urubú   TG, TU
Sanumã   YA
Nambiquára   NB
Mamaindé   NB

By examining the above classification, I come up with the following tentative statistics. Out of 24 of Brazil's indigenous languages:

  15 are quantity insensitive
  8 are quantity sensitive
  16 use end rule [final] (13 at foot level, all 16 at word level)
  5 use end rule [initial] (3 at foot level, 4 at word level)
  6 use perfect grid
  5 use QS rule
  8 appear to use some type of extrametricality
  9 appear to have stress applying in lexical component
  1 has no stress at all

The most obvious conclusion to be drawn from the above data is that there is a strong tendency toward quantity insensitive languages in Brazil. There is also a predominant use of the end rule final stress rule in the application of stress. These appear to be common tendencies which are found in many other parts of the world as well.

Of more particular interest to this study is the discovery that of the five languages which use the QS rule, three of them are tonal (Mura-Pirahã, Nambiquára, and Mamaindé). Could there be a link between tonal languages and quantity sensitivity? Using Goldsmith's idea of licensing, it would make sense that if a language allows a coda position to license an additional tone, creating contour tones, it would also allow the coda position to license an extra mora, creating heavy syllables. This similarity between the behavior of tonal systems and quantity sensitive stress systems is a matter to be investigated further.

I turn now to consider whether there are any general tendencies found within these particular language families in regard to stress placement. In the following tabulation, the number of total languages which have been included in the database from each particular language family is noted after the name of each family. I am aware that for most of these families, the number of languages studied here is only a fraction of the total number found within that family. Therefore any conclusions drawn from this small representative group are simply intended as suggestions for further research. Note also that six of the language families found in the previous pages are missing from the following list (the Guaikuru, Yanomami, Kamakan, Arawan, Maku, and Mura families). This is because my data includes only one language from each of these six families, making family generalizations impossible.

Tendencies by language family

Tupi (TU) family (5 total in database)
    All are quantity insensitive.
    All have ER [final, word].
    3 have ER [final, foot].
    2 have PG, peak first, foot level.

Je (JE) family (5 total in database)
    4 are quantity insensitive.
    1 is quantity sensitive.
    3 have ER [final, foot] and ER [final, word].
    2 have PG, peak first, R-L.

Carib (CA) family (4 total in database)
    2 are quantity sensitive.
    2 are quantity insensitive.
    All use ER [final, foot] and ER [final, word].

Arawak (AK) family (2 total in database)
    1 is quantity sensitive with ER [initial, foot].
    1 apparently has unpredictable stress.
    Both use stress for syntactic purposes.

Nambiquára (NB) family (2 total in database)
    Both are quantity sensitive.
    1 has ER [final, foot] and ER [final, word] as well as
    ER [initial, foot].
    1 apparently has unpredictable stress.
    Both use morpheme category to influence stress.

Some of these statistics merely restate the tendencies noted earlier. The Tupi-Guaraní and Je families, for example, seem to prefer quantity insensitivity. Tupi-Guaraní, Je, and Carib families also tend to favor the ER [final] stress rule. A much more detailed study by Rodrigues (1984, 1985) confirms this hypothesis for the Tupi-Guaraní language family. He lists over forty TG languages in his paper, noting that all but three of them stress the last syllable of the word, preserving the original form of the protolanguage. These three irregular languages, however, stress the penultimate syllable. By using metrical theory, one can posit that Proto Tupi employs end rule [final] to apply stress. Then it would not be very difficult to imagine that these three irregular languages could have undergone a simple diachronic change, by which they came to consider the last syllable as extrametrical. The advantage of this approach is that we can still say that these languages have maintained the original Tupi stress rule—ER [final]—which stresses the last syllable of a string. It is simply the case that in these three languages, the stress rule has become blind to the existence of the very last syllable, and therefore places the stress on the penultimate syllable.

The Arawak family, represented by Parecís and Terêna in the database, demonstrates a rather different tendency. In both of these languages, stress appears to be used for a variety of syntactic functions, such as to mark possession on nouns, which is typically carried out by additive morphology in other Brazilian languages. It would be interesting to discover whether this is a trait of the Arawak family or only of these two particular languages.

One last item to note about these language families is that, of the five languages in the database which employ the quantity sensitive rule, four of them come from only two language families; two from the Carib family and two from the Nambiquára family, of which Mamaindé is a part. Since the Nambiquára family is composed of only a total of three languages, it is safe to conclude that this is a predominantly quantity sensitive language family. The number of other languages within the Carib family which are quantity sensitive remains to be seen. All other language families had only one language represented as quantity sensitive and therefore no conclusions can be made about them.

Clearly, Brazil's languages show a great diversity of stress systems. I believe that in many of these languages, as in Mamaindé, stress is one of the basic underpinnings of the phonology; a quick glance at their phonology shows rules which can be formulated only by making reference to stressed segments. In Mamaindé, as mentioned earlier, the nasal spreading rule must make reference to the stressed syllable; stress in some sense supercedes nasality in the phonology. The same is true in many of the other languages, where another prosody must follow stress rules, whether it be nasality, laryngealization, length, tone, etc.

Besides being used as a conditioning factor for other phonological rules, stress may serve other purposes in these languages. In Xavánte, it marks constituent structure, such as feet, words, and phrases; in others (Urubú as well as Mamaindé) it marks morpheme classes, which helps in making decisions as to morpheme categories; in still others (such as Terêna) it marks grammatical categories.

Metrical phonology, and the nonlinear notions of autosegmental phonology (including the crucial idea of licensing), offer the means not only to describe these stress systems in precise, universally documented ways, but also to give a better understanding of how other prosodic features such as tone, nasalization, and laryngealization relate to stress (keeping in mind that in this paper I treat stress as an autosegment as well).

Lexical phonology, in turn, can give a better understanding of the organization of phonology and morphology in some of these languages and how stress fits into the overall picture of the phonology. In fact, I believe that in a few of these languages, Mamaindé being one of them, stress may be predicted only by making use of the notion of lexical strata. The nine languages listed in category 5 above are other possible candidates for a lexical approach to stress. It could be that Mamaindé is

Appendix 153

not alone among the languages of Brazil in its utilization of several strata in order to apply stress to a given word.

A larger question relating to lexical phonology and Brazilian languages is whether polysynthetic languages might have a tendency to use multiple lexical strata in their phonologies, and particularly in their stress rules. Mamaindé is highly polysynthetic since it commonly uses five or six morphemes per word, and can allow seven morphemes per word in unelicited speech, with many morpheme boundary rules applying at each juncture. Furthermore, the phonology must contain at least four strata. This seems to be a logical relationship, for as words grow longer by affixation processes, it seems natural that the phonology would provide multiple strata to consider these long strings in shorter chunks. It would assign different rules to each strata, effectively distinguishing between morpheme categories by means of phonological rules (including stress rules) instead of by means of word boundaries. This possible function of strata within a polysynthetic language is an interesting hypothesis which should be investigated further. (So far, Mamaindé and possibly Nambiquára hold promise for this hypothesis, but it is not clear whether the other languages in category 5 support this theory.)

It becomes apparent, then, that more of these languages should be studied in the light of these current theories of phonology. Up to now I have only found work by one other linguist, Everett (1988, 1990, 1992), which unites some of these newer phonology theories with Brazilian indigenous languages. I am convinced there is more to be learned about the phonology of this vast smorgasbord of Amazonian languages, just as there is in Mamaindé.

My purpose in this paper has been to show that these new phonological theories provide tools to explain more clearly Mamaindé stress phenomena—likewise, the Mamaindé data makes some relevant contributions and proposes some valid modifications to these theories.

I have argued that Mamaindé is best analyzed with two foot level rules, stress rules that spread over four strata, full grid copying, and the superiority of grids over trees for at least this language. Likewise, I believe that many other contributions to the study of stress could be made by other Brazilian languages. For example, Terêna shows stress as a function of grammar; Pirahã shows ternary feet, and onsets and voicing as a factor in defining heavy syllables; Urubú seems to show another stratal approach to stress; Apalaí shows interesting examples of stress clash; Xavánte shows an ideal example of mora counting in perfect grid. In short, almost every conceivable type of stress system is found among these languages.

In the past, adequate tools for describing complex stress systems were not fully developed. Today we have available several consistent methods, used extensively and successfully elsewhere around the world, which can possibly uncover some of the basic foundations of Amazonian languages. But as I have argued, not only could these new phonological theories result in better understanding of these languages, by the same token these languages could also contribute significant data that might stretch the limits of these theories and thus better our understanding of human language behavior as a whole.

References for languages listed in this appendix

Apalaí (Koehn 1986)
Apinayé (Callow 1962)
Asuriní (Harrison 1975)
Banawá (Buller and Everett 1992; Everett 1990)
Canela (Popjes 1986)
Guajajára (Bendor-Samuel 1972)
Hixkaryána (Derbyshire 1979 and 1985)
Kadiwéu (Griffiths and Griffiths 1976)
Kamã (Everett 1990)
Kamakan (Loukotka 1932)
Kamayurá (Saelzer 1976)
Kayapó (Stout and Thompson 1974)
Kradahó (Wilbert 1964)
Macushi (Hawkins 1950)
Maxakalí (Popovich 1985)
Mura-Pirahã (Everett 1988)
Nambiquára (Kroeker 1972; Kroeker 1976)
Parecís (Rowan 1967)
Sanumã (Borgman 1990)
Terêna (Bendor-Samuel 1963)
Uáiuái (Hawkins 1952)
Urubú (Kakumasu 1976 and 1986)
Wayampí (Jensen 1989)
Xavánte (McLeod and Mitchell 1977)

References

Anderson, Stephen R. 1984. A metrical interpretation of some traditional claims about quantity and stress. In Mark Aranoff and Richard Oehrle (eds.), Language sound structure: Studies in phonology presented to Morris Halle by his teacher and students. Cambridge: MIT Press.

Bendor-Samuel, David. 1972. Hierarchical structures in Guajajara. Publications in linguistics 37. Norman, Okla.: Summer Institute of Linguistics and the University of Oklahoma.

Bendor-Samuel, John T. 1963. Stress in Terena. Transactions of the Philological Society for 1962, 105–23. Oxford: Philological Society.

Bloomfield, Leonard. [1933] 1984. Language. Reprint. Chicago: University of Chicago Press.

Borgman, Donald M. 1990. Sanumã. In Desmond C. Derbyshire and Geoffrey K. Pullum (eds.), Handbook of Amazonian languages, 2:15–248. Berlin: Mouton.

Buller, Barbara, Ernest Buller, and Daniel L. Everett. 1992. Stress placement, syllable structure, and minimality in Banawá. ms.

Callow, John Campbell. 1962. The Apinayé language, phonology and grammar. Ph.D. dissertation. London University.

Camara, J. Mattoso Jr. 1965. Introdução às línguas indígenas brasileiras. Rio de Janeiro: Livraria Academica.

Chung, Sandra. 1983. Transderivational relationships in Chamorro phonology. Language 59:35–66.

Clements, George N. 1985. The geometry of phonological features. Phonology Yearbook 2:223–52.

Crystal, David. 1985. A dictionary of linguistics and phonetics. Oxford: Basil Blackwell.
Derbyshire, Desmond C. 1979. Hixkaryana. Lingua Descriptive Studies 1. Amsterdam: North-Holland.
———. 1985. Hixkaryana and linguistic typology. Publications in Linguistics 76. Dallas: Summer Institute of Linguistics and the University of Texas at Arlington.
Eberhard, David. 1992. Mamaindé reduplication in the autosegmental model. ms.
———. 1993. Nasal prosody in Mamaindé. ms.
Everett, Daniel L. 1986. Ternarity and obligatory branching in Pirahã. In Desmond Derbyshire (ed.), Work papers of the Summer Institute of Linguistics. University of North Dakota 30:13–41.
———. 1988. On metrical constituent structure in Pirahã phonology. Natural Language and Language Theory 6:207–46.
———. 1990. Extraprosodicity and minimality in Kamã and Banawá. University of Pittsburgh Working Papers in Linguistics.1. Pittsburgh.
———. 1992. On subsyllabic feet and the mora in Kamã. ms.
Garvin, Paul L. 1948. Esquisse du systeme phonologique du nambikwara-tarunde. Journal de la Societé des Americanistes, Nouvelle Série. 37:133–89.
Giegerich, Heinz J. 1985. Metrical phonology and phonological structure: German and English. London: Cambridge University Press.
Goldsmith, John A. 1976. Autosegmental phonology. Bloomington: Indiana University Linguistics Club.
———. 1990. Autosegmental and metrical phonology. Oxford: Basil Blackwell.
Griffiths, Glyndwr and Cynthia Griffiths. 1976. Aspectos da lingua kadiwéu. Série Linguistica 6. Brasília: Summer Institute of Linguistics.
Halle, Morris and Jean-Roger Vergnaud. 1987. An essay on stress. Cambridge: MIT Press.
Harris, James W. 1982. Spanish syllable structure and stress: A nonlinear analysis. Linguistic Inquiry Monograph 8. Cambridge: MIT Press.
Harrison, Carl H. 1975. Gramática asuriní: Aspectos de una gramática transformacional e discursos monologados da lingua asuriní, familia tupi guaraní. Série Linguistica 4:171–72. Brasília: Summer Institute of Linguistics.
Hawkins, W. Neil. 1950. Patterns of vowel loss in Macushi (Carib). International Journal of American Linguistics 16:

——. 1952. A fonologia da língua uáiuái. Etnografia e Tupi-guaraní 25, Boletim 157. São Paulo: Universidade de Saõ Paulo.
Hayes, Bruce Philip. 1981. A metrical theory of stress rules. Bloomington: Indiana University Linguistics Club.
Jensen, Cheryl Joyce S. 1989. O desenvolvimento historico da lingua wayampi. Campinas, Brazil: Editora da UNICAMP.
Kakumasu, James Y. 1976. Gramática gerativa preliminar da lingua urubú. Série Linguistica 5:171-97. Summer Institute of Linguistics.
——. 1986. Urubu-Kaapor. In Desmond C. Derbyshire and Geoffrey K. Pullum (eds.), Handbook of Amazonian Languages, 1:326-403. Berlin: Mouton.
Kaufman, Terrence. 1990. Language history in South America: What we know and how to know more. In Doris L. Payne (ed.), Amazonian linguistics: Studies in lowland South American languages, 13-73. Austin: University Press of Texas.
Kingston, Peter. 1971. Mamaindé verbs. ms.
——. 1976. Sufixos referenciais e o elemento nominal na língua mamaindé. Série Linguistica 5:31-81. Brasília: Summer Institute of Linguistics.
——. 1976. Morpheme boundary phenomenon in Mamaindé. ms.
——. 1991a. Dicionario mamaindé-portugues/portugues-mamaindé, experimental edition. Cuiabá, Brazil: Summer Institute of Linguistics.
——. 1991b. Grammatica pedagogica mamaindé. ms.
——. n.d. Mamaindé syllables. ms.
——. n.d. Mamaindé phonology. ms.
——. n.d. Some notes on Mamaindé morphology and morphophonemics. ms.
——. n.d. Tonal configurations and perturbation in Mamaindé. ms.
——. n.d. Tonal curves and perturbation in Mamaindé. ms.
Kiparsky, Paul. 1973. Elsewhere in phonology. In Stephen Anderson and Paul Kiparsky (eds.), A festschrift for Morris Halle. New York: Holt Rinehart and Winston.
——. 1982. Lexical morphology and phonology. In I. S. Yang (ed.), Linguistics in the morning calm. Seoul: Hanshin.
Koehn, Edward and Sally S. Koehn. 1986. Apalai. In Desmond C. Derbyshire and Geoffrey K. Pullum (eds.), Handbook of Amazonian Languages, 1:33-127. Berlin: Mouton.
Kroeker, Barbara J. 1972. Morphophonemics of Nambiquara. Anthropological Linguistics 14:19-22.

Kroeker, Menno. 1976. Condicionamento múltiplo de vogais na lingua Nambikuara. Série Linguistica 5:107–30. Brasília: Summer Institute of Linguistics.

Lester, Peter F. 1994. Altered states: A Study of Waorani (Auca) stress. M.A. thesis. University of Texas at Arlington.

Liberman, Mark and Alan Prince. 1977. On stress and linguistic rhythm. Linguistic Inquiry 8:249–336.

Loukotka, Chestmir. 1932. La familia linguistica kamakan del brasil. Revista del Instituto de Etnologia 2. Tucumán, Argentina: Universidad Nacional de Tucumán.

Marantz, A. 1982. Re-reduplication. Linguistic Inquiry 13:435–982.

McLeod, Ruth and Valerie Mitchell. 1977. Aspectos da lingua xavánte. Brasília: Summer Institute of Linguistics.

McQuown, Norman and Joseph Greenberg. 1960. Sol Tax, aboriginal languages of Latin America. Current Anthropology 1:431–36.

Mohanan, K. P. 1986. The theory of lexical phonology. Dordrecht, Holland: D. Reidel.

Payne, Doris. 1990. Morphological characteristics of lowland South American languages. In Doris L. Payne (ed.). Amazonian linguistics: Studies in lowland South American languages, 213–41. Austin: University Press of Texas.

Popjes, Jack and Josephine Popjes. 1986. Canela-Krahô. In Desmond C. Derbyshire and Geoffrey K. Pullum (eds.), Handbook of Amazonian languages, 1:128–99. Berlin: Mouton.

Popovich, Andrew Harold. 1985. Discourse phonology of Maxakalí: A multilevel, multiunit approach. M.A. thesis. University of Texas at Arlington.

Price, David. n.d. Southern Nambiquara phonology. ms.

Prince, Alan S. 1984. Relating to the grid. Linguistic Inquiry 14:19–100.

Ribeiro, Darcy. 1957. Línguas e culturas indígenas do brasil. Educação e Ciencias Sociais 6. Rio de Janeiro: Centro Brasileiro de Pesquisas Educacionais.

Rodrigues, Aryon Dall'Igna. 1963. Os estudos de linguistica indigena no brasil. Revista de Antropologia 11. São Paulo: Universidade de São Paulo.

———. 1984/1985. Relações internas na familia linguistica tupiguarani. Revista de Antropologia 27, 28. São Paulo: Universidade de São Paulo.

———. 1986. Línguas Brasileiras: Para o conhecimento das línguas indígenas. São Paulo: Edições Loyola.

Bibliography

Rowan, Orland. 1967. Phonology of Paresí (Arawakan). Acta Linguistica Hafniensia 10(2). Copenhagen.

Saelzer, Meinke. 1976. Fonologia provisória da língua kamayurá. Serie Linguistica 5:131–70. Brasília: Summer Institute of Linguistics.

Stout, Mickey and Ruth Thomson. 1974. Fonémica txukuhamẽi (kayapó). Série Linguistica 3:153–76. Brasília: Summer Institute of Linguistics.

Voegelin, C. F. and F. M. Voegelin. 1977. Classification and index of the world's languages. New York: Elsevier.

Wilbert, Johannes. 1964. Material linguistica ye. Caracas, Venezuela: Editorial Sucre.

Willett, Elizabeth. 1982. Reduplication and accent in southeastern Tepehuan. International Journal of American Linguistics 48:168–84.

www.ingramcontent.com/pod-product-compliance
Lightning Source LLC
Chambersburg PA
CBHW070333230426
43663CB00011B/2295